ISSUE 12, JULY 2021

AUSTRALIAN FOREIGN AFFAIRS

Contributors

Allan Behm is the director of international and security affairs at the Australia Institute.

Anthony Bergin is a senior fellow with the Australian Strategic Policy Institute.

David Brophy is a senior lecturer in Modern Chinese History at the University of Sydney.

Richard Denniss is the chief economist at the Australia Institute.

Amanda McKenzie is the CEO and co-founder of The Climate Council.

Wesley Morgan is a research fellow at the Griffith Asia Institute at Griffith University.

Hugh Riminton is national affairs editor at Network Ten and a former reporter and news presenter for CNN.

Michelle Aung Thin is a novelist, essayist and senior lecturer at RMIT University and the author of several novels.

Jeffrey Wall has been a senior adviser on Papua New Guinea and a consultant to the World Bank.

Marian Wilkinson is a Walkley Award–winning journalist and author of *The Carbon Club*.

Australian Foreign Affairs is published three times a year by Schwartz Books Pty Ltd. Publisher: Morry Schwartz. ISBN 978-1-76064-2112 ISSN 2208-5912 ALL RIGHTS RESERVED. No part of this publication may be reproduced, stored in a retrieval system, or transmitted in any form by any means, electronic, mechanical, photocopying, recording or otherwise, without the prior consent of the publishers. Essays, reviews and correspondence © retained by the authors. Subscriptions – 1 year print & digital auto-renew (3 issues): $49.99 within Australia incl. GST. 1 year print and digital subscription (3 issues): $59.99 within Australia incl. GST. 2 year print & digital (6 issues): $114.99 within Australia incl. GST. 1 year digital only auto-renew: $29.99. Payment may be made by MasterCard, Visa or Amex, or by cheque made out to Schwartz Books Pty Ltd. Payment includes postage and handling. To subscribe, fill out the form inside this issue, subscribe online at www.australianforeignaffairs.com, email subscribe@australianforeignaffairs.com or phone 1800 077 514 / 61 3 9486 0288. Correspondence should be addressed to: The Editor, Australian Foreign Affairs, Level 1, 221 Drummond Street, Carlton VIC 3053 Australia Phone: 61 3 9486 0288 / Fax: 61 3 9486 0244 Email: enquiries@australianforeignaffairs.com Editor: Jonathan Pearlman. Deputy Editor: Julia Carlomagno. Associate Editor: Chris Feik. Consulting Editor: Allan Gyngell. Digital Editor and Marketing: Amy Rudder. Editorial Intern: Lachlan McIntosh. Management: Elisabeth Young. Subscriptions: Iryna Byelyayeva and Sam Perazzo. Publicity: Anna Lensky. Design: Peter Long. Production Coordination and Typesetting: Tristan Main. Cover photographs by Ed Connor / Shutterstock (clouds) and Kelly Barnes / AAP (Morrison). Printed in Australia by McPherson's Printing Group.

FEELING THE HEAT

Australia has always taken a shrewd, calculating approach to pursuing prosperity and influence in a world in which it is not powerful enough – alone – to guarantee its own security or to change the global order.

Its method is to sidle up to wealthier and stronger partners, and to support a set of international rules and bodies that make it harder for the most powerful nations to impose their will on others. This approach has led to Australia's close ties to countries such as the United States, Japan and the United Kingdom, and to its vocal support – expressed at every opportunity by successive foreign ministers – for promoting the "rules-based order".

But there is a glaring exception to the nation's practice of its own well-worn foreign policy.

In recent years, as the need to address climate change has shifted to the centre of the international agenda, Australia has stayed still. Its reluctance to act is now putting it at odds with both its allies, and with the system of international rule-making.

The world has reached a consensus around the need for collective action on climate change. Despite the deteriorating ties between the United States and China, and their continued trade war, the two countries issued a joint statement on the climate crisis in April and committed to "raising global climate ambition". Both Joe Biden and Xi Jinping have committed to a net-zero emissions target. According to the London-based Energy and Climate Intelligence Unit, 132 countries have now adopted or are considering adopting net-zero emissions targets. The list includes South Korea, Germany, France, Brazil, Somalia, Lebanon and Laos – but not Australia.

The Coalition's current stance – particularly its resistance to stronger carbon emission reduction targets – is not just an evasion of science. It also undercuts Australia's ties with its closest partners, and its Pacific step-up, and its potential to steer the new global clean economy. It is a failure of foreign policy.

Former prime minister Malcolm Turnbull recently summed up this failure during an event at the Lowy Institute: "We are more out of step on climate with the rest of the world and in particular our closest friends and allies than we have ever been on any big international issue."

In April this year, Biden convened a climate summit and declared: "The cost of inaction keeps mounting. The United States isn't waiting." Xi, in attendance, called for "common progress in the new journey toward global carbon neutrality". As the European Union, the United Kingdom, Canada and others all promised stronger emissions reduction targets, Prime Minister Scott Morrison made no new commitments and relied instead on his government's much-disputed claim that it is on track to meet its targets promised under the Paris Agreement.

He told the summit: "Future generations will thank us not for what we have promised, but what we deliver."

But Morrison's stance is a rejection of the international community's approach to tackling climate change. The push for stronger targets was not the sudden consequence of a more progressive candidate winning last year's US election. It was always intended that the Paris Agreement would establish initial targets, and that countries would then strengthen them.

At the upcoming climate conference in Glasgow in November, countries will present plans for achieving these stronger targets. Australia will need to decide whether it wants to pursue a climate policy that accords with the international consensus, or to undermine the foreign policy that has, for so long, guaranteed its stability and security.

Australia is under pressure to act. The appeals from its partners are genuine, as are the threats of sanctions and retribution. Its options and opportunities need to be understood, as do the consequences of inaction. Australia's climate policy is not just a matter of domestic debate – it is an indispensable part of the nation's foreign affairs.

Jonathan Pearlman

THE OUTLIER

Morrison's world-defying climate stance

Marian Wilkinson

Lesley Hughes doesn't get a lot of invitations from the Morrison government to sit at the top table. The high-profile climate scientist was unceremoniously sacked, along with the entire Climate Commission, shortly after Tony Abbott became prime minister. His successors have shunned her advice ever since. So it was surprising to see Professor Hughes on stage in Sydney as a guest speaker at a climate leadership event organised by the British consulate general to celebrate this year's International Women's Day.

As the invitees tucked into breakfast at The Mint museum, Hughes was quizzed on the looming climate crisis by Sam Mostyn, president of Chief Executive Women and networker extraordinaire. Joining them on stage were a feisty grassroots climate activist and the CEO of a start-up that offsets personal carbon footprints.

It was a small but revealing display of British diplomacy in the lead-up to November's critical United Nations Climate Change Conference in Glasgow (COP26). And Hughes was happy to be part of it. "It's soft pressure, obviously," she said later, "but it's nonetheless a demonstration of the importance of the issue."

Hughes was a lead author on the landmark Fifth Assessment Report by the Intergovernmental Panel on Climate Change (IPCC). The report helped guide the Paris Agreement and its aim to limit global warming to below 2 degrees Celsius, and preferably to 1.5, compared to pre-industrial levels. Hughes now regularly issues warnings about the climate crisis through the Climate Council – an independent body known for its sharp criticism of the Morrison government's unambitious targets to cut Australia's greenhouse emissions.

The professor's appearance at the British event was just one more line item in the United Kingdom's effort to pull off the world's most ambitious climate summit yet in Glasgow. The measure of the summit's success will not just be a commitment to reach a global target of net-zero emissions by 2050. To make that target credible, British prime minister Boris Johnson and his cabinet colleague Alok Sharma, COP26 president-designate, want all countries – especially developed countries such as Australia – to commit to ambitious targets for 2030, just nine years away. That outcome is also a top priority for US president Joe Biden. The new 2030 targets and the plans to achieve them will need to be submitted to the United Nations as Nationally Determined Contributions (NDCs), as required under the Paris Agreement.

"We've asked all countries coming to Glasgow to be ambitious," British high commissioner Vicki Treadell said in an interview with Australian Foreign Affairs. The United Kingdom has already committed to emissions-reduction targets of 68 per cent by 2030 and 78 per cent by 2035. "We're pleased to see the changing language here in Australia and certainly the commitment from Prime Minister Morrison that they recognise the need to get to net zero, in his words, preferably by 2050," she said, but added pointedly, "What we do want to understand is how people are going to measure their success and the way they are going to get there with the initial plans for 2030. And then between 2030 and 2050, what that final push will be."

Since last December, Scott Morrison has crab-walked towards a net zero by 2050 target. But he's come under pressure from Australia's most important allies to put up a credible 2030 target in Glasgow. Morrison has been unwilling to do that. Why?

Australia's rocky path to Glasgow

Australia's current 2030 target was set six years ago by Tony Abbott's cabinet and signed off by the Coalition party room in the lead-up to the Paris negotiations. The target, to cut emissions between 26 and 28 per cent below 2005 levels, has Australia on track to remain one of the highest per-capita greenhouse emitters in the developed world, alongside Russia and Saudi Arabia.

Abbott's successor, Malcolm Turnbull, was unable to change the target. As Turnbull put it after he was dumped as prime minister,

Australia's climate and energy policy was a toxic time bomb, "ticking away in the prime minister's desk drawer". Now Morrison, feeling the heat from Australia's allies, from growing numbers in the business community and from a majority of voters, needs to work out how he will handle that bomb.

So far, the prime minister has signalled he wants to stick with an unambitious policy and avoid a blow-up in the Coalition party room, even if it means staring down London and Washington. While he is prepared to move gingerly towards the 2050 target before Glasgow, government sources insist a new 2030 target is off the table. Both Morrison and his energy and emissions reductions minister, Angus Taylor, made the weak 2030 target an election commitment in 2019. When Labor campaigned to reduce emissions by 45 per cent by 2030 and to boost renewable energy, Taylor called it "reckless" and "a wrecking ball through the economy".

Taylor has strong support for his approach from many on the Coalition's right. Liberal Party moderates are also reluctant to press the case to increase the 2030 target, fearing it will unleash internal ructions and destabilise the government. Despite his initial success in managing the COVID-19 pandemic, Morrison's mishandling of the sex scandals in Parliament House, followed by the flawed vaccine roll-out, raised anxiety levels in party ranks earlier this year. The forced resignation of Liberal Party climate sceptic Craig Kelly in March left the government with just enough votes to control the House. Adding to Morrison's woes, his Coalition partners, the Nationals, are bitterly divided over their leader, Michael McCormack. Revisiting the emissions targets could be used as another excuse to blow up McCormack's leadership, causing more grief for the government.

Morrison is relying heavily on Angus Taylor as he charts Australia's increasingly rocky path to Glasgow. The minister is pushing his vaunted Low Emissions Technology Investment Roadmap – with its mantra "technology not taxes" – as the centrepiece of the government's long-term emissions-reduction strategy. His plan locks in small emissions cuts until 2030, while promising big cuts between 2030 and 2050 and beyond, based on future clean technology breakthroughs. Taylor argues, "the only pathway to global emissions reduction while strengthening prosperity is through developing low-emissions technologies at a lower cost than higher-emitting alternatives."

In effect, the roadmap is a promise to the Liberal Party's right wing and to the Nationals that the government will not return to the Rudd–Gillard policies of putting a price on greenhouse emissions. But without a carbon price, there is no price signal to drive a more rapid shift to a clean energy economy.

The policy of small steps to 2030 is squarely aimed at holding Coalition seats in regional Australia. Taylor and Morrison have used it to give their full-throttled support to "a gas-led recovery" and new investment in the gas industry in Queensland, New South Wales and Western Australia. Taylor also backs a role for coal "for many years to come". At the same time, Morrison and Taylor are trying to reassure the nation that the roadmap will deliver the long-term solution to the climate crisis. The government has put up big licks of money for research and development into future projects, including a hydrogen export hub, long-duration battery storage, pilot carbon capture and storage sites, low-emissions steel and aluminium production, along with soil carbon programs for farmers to make money trading carbon credits with big greenhouse-gas-emitting businesses.

The roadmap brushes aside one crucial development – the IPCC Special Report on Global Warming of 1.5°C. The report found the initial Paris targets would not deliver the emissions reductions necessary to keep the goal of 1.5 degrees within reach, and said a rapid and far-reaching energy transformation was needed. While the modelling was complex and qualified, the take-home message was that the world needed to cut CO_2 emissions nearly in half by 2030 and get to net zero by 2050.

When that report was released in 2018, Morrison had been prime minister for just over a month. Questioned about its ominous findings, he dismissed the report by saying it didn't have special recommendations for Australia and was "dealing with the global program". Many Coalition backbenchers and some in the cabinet regarded the IPCC's climate scientists as alarmist.

Neither Morrison nor Taylor took seriously the idea that the 1.5-degree goal would determine global energy policy. They stuck to the earlier modelling for Paris that looked at the world reaching net zero in the second half of this century. At the time, Donald Trump was in the White House and the United States was set to withdraw from the Paris

Agreement. As a result, it looked highly unlikely that China, the world's largest greenhouse-gas emitter, would agree to speed up its emissions reductions to achieve the Paris goal.

In a withering analysis, Hughes and her colleagues at the Climate Council castigated the Morrison government's response to the IPCC report. "The tension between the need for urgent action and ideologically driven denialism and inaction is evident in Australia," they wrote. "The window of opportunity to effectively tackle climate change is closing fast. We need to rapidly and deeply cut our emissions."

That didn't happen. Instead, on 22 September 2020, the Morrison government launched its roadmap. Taylor described it as "a plan that would bring the world with us". But

> **Every G7 country was set to commit to the 2050 goal. But Morrison baulked at joining them**

it was a policy designed for the Trump era, and was overrun by global events less than a day after Taylor unveiled it. While the minister was laying out his plans for modest support for long-term research and development in clean technology, President Xi Jinping was preparing to give a speech that would reset the international climate negotiations.

Global pressure builds

In a virtual address to the United Nations General Assembly on the same day the Coalition's roadmap was released, Xi stunned the world by announcing China would set a target of reaching net-zero emissions before 2060. He also reconfirmed China's goal to peak its carbon dioxide emissions before 2030.

Despite deep cynicism from some observers in Australia, Xi's announcement was "a big surprise that sent a pretty big market signal", according to Sam Geall, a UK specialist in China's environment policy with think tank China Dialogue.

Significantly, one week before his net-zero pledge, Xi had held a tense video conference with German chancellor Angela Merkel, president of the European Council Charles Michel and president of the European Commission Ursula von der Leyen. On the table were China's climate policy and negotiations for an EU–China Comprehensive Agreement on Investment. Among the concessions being sought by the European Union was a signal from China that it would strengthen its commitment on peaking its carbon dioxide emissions by 2030 and setting a goal to reach net zero.

Xi's announcement was a breakthrough for the EU, but it also allowed China to reposition itself as a lead player in the global climate negotiations, in stark contrast to Trump. China's relationship with the United States was in freefall, making a breakthrough agreement with Europe all the more important.

The EU's ambassador to Australia, Dr Michael Pulch, told Australian Foreign Affairs there were several reasons for the timing of Xi's announcement, including soaring concerns among China's urban middle class over air pollution. But he agreed the relationship with Europe did "come into play". Xi's move sent a crucial signal that the global climate talks, sidelined by the pandemic and Trump, would get back on track. As Pulch explained, "it would become so much more difficult to get everyone engaged if there was a question mark over China's policy, given the huge percentage of emissions that come from a country like China."

A month after Xi's announcement, two of Australia's biggest trading partners, Japan and South Korea, pledged carbon neutrality by 2050. "When you create a momentum then it often drives everyone forward," said Pulch. "We suddenly had that momentum."

Just a fortnight later, in November, Joe Biden was elected president on the most ambitious climate policy in US history. Promising to rejoin the Paris Agreement, Biden also committed to net-zero emissions by 2050. Describing climate change as "an existential threat", Biden called for America to "lead the world in addressing the climate emergency" and argued this would happen with a clean energy revolution at home. Central to Biden's policy was a promise to America's blue-collar unions that jobs would flow from this green revolution.

Hard on the heels of Biden's election, Canada's prime minister, Justin Trudeau, also pledged a target of net-zero emissions by 2050. By November 2020, every G7 country – France, Germany, Italy, Japan, the United Kingdom, the United States and Canada – was set to commit to the 2050 goal. Together, they accounted for around 40 per cent of the world's GDP. But Scott Morrison baulked at joining them. That's when the pressure on the Australian prime minister began to ratchet up.

The energy revolution

In December 2020, Boris Johnson hosted a virtual climate summit with the United Nations' secretary-general, António Guterres, after the pandemic had forced the delay of COP26 to 2021. The UK government had written to heads of state inviting them to attend but, according to Vicki Treadell, leaders had to guarantee to meet specific criteria if they were to address the summit. "The annexes to the letter of invitation set out very clearly that an ambitious net-zero target by 2050 and more ambitious NDCs [Nationally Determined Contributions] would be required to meet the bar for a speaking slot," she said.

Morrison would not make that commitment. After a flurry of diplomatic activity, Alok Sharma delivered the bad news to Angus Taylor that Morrison hadn't made the speakers' cut. Morrison's offer of a "clean technology partnership" with the United Kingdom and a long-delayed concession not to use so-called "carryover credits" from the Kyoto Agreement to reach its weak 2030 target were not enough to sway Johnson.

Writing to Morrison on 8 December, Johnson explained his decision to exclude him and made clear he expected Morrison to do better before Glasgow – even though he understood the politics were fraught: "I welcome your personal commitment to Net Zero, and look forward to Australia setting a time bound commitment and an ambitious Nationally Determined Contribution next year ... I recognise how complex these issues are domestically and your own personal stake in this."

In February 2021, two months after this rebuff, Morrison finally got to his feet at the National Press Club to announce his government's goal was to reach net-zero emissions "as soon as possible, and preferably by 2050". It was still not a commitment – just a goal – and Morrison quickly reverted to Taylor's mantra of "technology not taxes", insisting that his government would "not tax our way to net-zero emissions".

But Morrison and Taylor were again overrun by events. The Biden administration was preparing to hold its own global climate summit in April and was drawing up plans for an ambitious 2030 target.

In an address in February, Biden's climate envoy, John Kerry, had homed in on the importance of the 2030 target to cut global emissions. "In order to meet the standard of what we have set for 2030, to meet the Paris standard and beyond, we have to now phase out coal five times faster than we have been," said Kerry. "We have to increase tree cover five times faster than we have been. We have to ramp up renewable energy six times faster than we are." On electric vehicles, Kerry warned, the transition needed was staggering – "a rate 22 times faster than we are today".

This speed was beyond the thinking inside the Morrison government. But in America, the European Union and the United Kingdom, many in big business were reading the signals that the Paris goal was real and the race for clean energy superiority was on.

Nowhere was this clearer than in the global car industry. Soon after Biden's inauguration, America's auto giant, General Motors, stunned the industry by announcing it would phase out petrol- and diesel-powered cars and trucks by 2035. GM was not just competing with Elon Musk's Tesla – by now, three Chinese electric vehicle companies had already been listed on the US stock exchange, while domestic Chinese carmakers were also gearing up for mass electric vehicle production.

The United Kingdom was also committed to stop selling new diesel and petrol cars from 2030 as part of its own technology roadmap, rolled out in November 2020. As Treadell put it, with the UK lobbying hard for ambitious targets in Glasgow, "we must in turn walk the talk ourselves".

Treadell argues that ambition is already paying off for post-Brexit Britain. "We are seeing with a target and a plan, industry responding to that and all the majors who manufacture cars in the UK confirming what they are going to do."

More surprising is the shift by European automakers, particularly in Germany, which had long resisted the move away from diesel cars. Despite his electric vehicle rollout plan being plagued with software problems, Volkswagen Group CEO Herbert Diess announced in March that "e-mobility has won the race". The German auto giant said it would have six "gigafactories" supplying battery cells in Europe by 2030.

The shift in Europe is being supercharged by its "green recovery" deal, sealed in 2020 as part of its post-pandemic stimulus. EU leaders agreed to devote nearly one-third of the EU budget and COVID-19 recovery package to green projects over the next seven years. "I think German industry saw the writing on the wall," said Pulch. "We decided we don't want to go back to where we were before ... and we'll use the pandemic basically to leapfrog to a different state of our economy. And that is happening. So the Volkswagen announcement came in that context. But you'll see it from other European producers."

Indeed, Swedish automaker Volvo announced it would start work this year on its first concept vehicles using "green" steel made with renewable energy and hydrogen by SSAB, the Nordic steel giant. Volvo today is a subsidiary of one of China's largest private carmakers, Zhejiang Geely Holding Group, founded by billionaire Li Shufu.

The huge disruption to global industries such as cars and steel explains why the European Union is moving quickly to impose carbon tariffs on its trading competitors. Europe has a carbon price, thanks to its emissions trading scheme, which

The economic impact of [a] shift to clean energy will hit Australia on multiple fronts

covers 40 per cent of its greenhouse gas emissions. Its member states don't want local businesses and labour unions up in arms over competition from imported goods made with cheap fossil fuels in China and India.

When the European Parliament voted overwhelmingly in March to impose the carbon tariffs, it sparked an angry reaction in Canberra. Australia's trade minister, Dan Tehan, slammed it as "protectionist". But the MEPs insisted a carbon price on key imports from less climate-ambitious countries was critical because "global climate efforts will not benefit if EU production is just moved to non-EU countries that have less ambitious emissions rules".

The European Union wants to have carbon tariffs in place by early 2023. In the short term, the tariffs will have a limited impact on Australia – agriculture, for example, will not be included. But Australia is right now negotiating its free trade agreement with the European Union. And while a net zero by 2050 target is not an explicit prerequisite, the EU and its member states would be unlikely to ratify an agreement without Australia's commitment to the target.

More worrying for the government, the Biden administration has warned it too will look at imposing carbon tariffs to protect its blue-collar workers and manufacturers if its trade competitors don't raise their climate ambitions. Pulch sees this as likely. "Those countries that have to decarbonise manufacturing will all look at something similar to make sure there continues to be a level playing field for their operators."

Carbon tariffs will put pressure not only on China but also on Japan, South Korea and India – Australia's big customers for coking coal, thermal coal and liquified natural gas. If these countries respond by cutting their emissions sharply this decade, the economic impact of their shift to clean energy will hit Australia on multiple fronts.

Domestic pressure

Both Morrison and Taylor are acutely aware the climate debate has moved on with Biden's election. That message is not coming just from Washington, London and Brussels but from senior Australian business figures. Publicly, high-tech billionaire and influential clean energy investor Mike Cannon-Brookes has thrown brickbats at Morrison and Taylor over their policy. Behind the scenes, Morrison's thinking has been shaken up by key business leaders, such as Macquarie Group's CEO, Shemara Wikramanayake, who sits on the government's Technology Investment Advisory Council, chaired by Dr Alan Finkel, Australia's former chief scientist. The Business Council of Australia, the Australian Industry Group and the National Farmers' Federation all moved ahead of the government in supporting the net zero by 2050 target.

Australian business knows the global energy industry is entering a period of rapid change, and so too are the financial markets. For investors, shareholders, banks, superannuation funds and financial regulators, climate risk is no longer theoretical – it's a reality that has to be calculated. But Australian business is conflicted as its fossil fuel executives, investors and union allies lobby to keep their influence. This was all too apparent when Morrison and Taylor trumpeted the "gas-led recovery" as part of Australia's response to the pandemic and backed Santos's big new gas development at Narrabri, in New South Wales. As a result, most big-business leaders have taken a softly-softly approach, steering away from publicly calling for an increase in Australia's 2030 target.

Among the notable exceptions is maverick mining billionaire Andrew "Twiggy" Forrest, who has joined Cannon-Brookes in investing

The government's reluctance to officially change its 2030 target appears to be political

in the Northern Territory renewable energy project Sun Cable. Forrest's carbon-intensive iron-ore company, Fortescue Metals Group, annually produces more emissions than the entire nation of Bhutan. In a radical move this year, Forrest announced Fortescue would become one of the world's biggest renewables and resources companies. Forrest is one of several major players hoping to pull off billion-dollar green hydrogen projects in Australia.

In a remarkable Boyer Lecture broadcast on the ABC in January, Forrest argued the world couldn't wait for 2050 because "our planet will be toast". Backing the scientific advice of aiming for a 1.5-degree limit to global warming, Forrest called for business and government to work together to accelerate the shift to clean energy.

Under pressure at home and abroad, Morrison and Taylor have still baulked at any serious change of policy. This is despite Taylor repeatedly stating that Australia's current 2030 target is "a floor, not a ceiling" and predicting we will "overachieve" it. Government sources agree, and say Australia could raise its 2030 target from a 26 per cent reduction to a 30–35 per cent reduction without great difficulty.

State and territory governments already have net-zero targets for 2050, and most are likely to make significant emissions reductions by 2030. The Victorian government is promising a 45–50 per cent target for 2030. In New South Wales, where Liberal state energy minister Matt Kean has launched his own energy roadmap, the target is 35 per cent reductions by 2030, and that is likely to get more ambitious. A lot of these reductions are expected to come from the electricity sector, where renewable energy is rapidly pushing down the price of electricity and squeezing out coal-fired generators. In New South Wales and Victoria, four big coal-fired power stations are expected to shut down by 2030, along with others in Queensland. This is despite Taylor's efforts to extend their life.

The reason for the government's reluctance to officially change its 2030 target for Glasgow appears to be political. The updates on emissions projections for 2030 that are expected to include the "overachievement" don't have to go to cabinet and to the party room. But changes to formal targets are another matter. To officially reset the 2030 target, Morrison and Taylor would likely have to reopen the policy debate with the Liberal right and the Nationals in cabinet and the party room on how a new target will be achieved and whether it is consistent with a net-zero target for 2050. That would in turn reignite the public and parliamentary debate with Labor, the Greens and the independents over whether the 2030 target should be closer to a 50 per cent reduction, in line with other developed countries, to reach the Paris goal.

Taylor admitted Australia's 2030 target was too weak to hit net zero by 2050 when he spoke with Radio National's Fran Kelly in November 2020. "We know that if you have a net-zero across the board 2050 target, your 2030 target will be around 43 per cent," said Taylor, "very close to what Labor took to the last election."

Also tricky for Taylor and Morrison is that the 2030 "overachievement" they trumpet relies heavily on big emissions reductions from falls in Australia's high rates of land clearing. But land-clearing regulations are still bitterly resented by many in the National Party. By contrast, emissions from transport, key manufacturing industries and LNG production continue to be stubbornly high, except for the hit they took in the pandemic.

The bottom line is whether Morrison can credibly announce a 2050 net-zero target before Glasgow without lifting the 2030 target. But lifting that target, and overhauling the roadmap, would create significant political problems and place a serious question mark over Taylor's job.

Decision time

Morrison's determination to stick to Australia's weak, increasingly implausible 2030 target came under serious pressure at President Biden's climate summit in April. The prime minister was one of forty world leaders, including Xi Jinping, who attended the virtual gathering. It was designed to vault the United States into a leadership role in the global climate negotiations, and in his opening remarks Biden made it absolutely clear he wanted deep global emissions cuts by 2030. "This is the decade we must make decisions that will avoid the worst consequences of a climate crisis," Biden said. "We must try to keep the Earth's temperature to an increase of 1.5 degrees Celsius."

Biden used his summit to unveil a new US 2030 target of 50–52 per cent reductions in emissions. Japan's prime minister, Yoshihide Suga, offered up a 46 per cent reduction target, and Trudeau put up 40–45 per cent. All were close to double Australia's 2030 target. But Morrison again declined to commit even to a net zero by 2050 target, let alone change Australia's 2030 target.

Before Morrison could put his case to the summit, a senior US administration official was briefing the media, suggesting Australia's strategy was unsustainable. "At the moment I think our colleagues in Australia recognise there is going to have to be a shift," the official said. "It's insufficient to follow the existing trajectory and hope that they will be on a course to deep decarbonisation and getting to net zero emissions by mid-century."

But when Morrison spoke, he stuck to the "technology not taxes" mantra and Australia's slower approach to reducing emissions. "Australia is on the pathway to net zero," he said. "Our goal is to get there as soon as we possibly can, through technology that enables and transforms our industries, not taxes that eliminate them and the jobs and livelihoods they support and create, especially in our regions. For Australia, it is not a question of if or even by when for net zero, but importantly, how."

To back up his argument, Morrison invoked Finkel, noting that the former chief scientist was now the government's special adviser on low-emissions technology and the roadmap. But as one former insider put it, Morrison cannot use Finkel as a human shield for his policy.

Morrison's argument of "how" not "when" Australia gets to net zero missed the point. For Biden, it is a question of when as well as how. This is not just about the climate science. The United States sees itself in a race against China for clean energy supremacy in the net-zero emissions world. Secretary of state Antony Blinken made this clear shortly before the Biden summit. "It's difficult to imagine the United States winning the long-term strategic competition with China if we cannot lead the renewable energy revolution," he told reporters. "Right now, we're falling behind. China is the largest producer and exporter of solar panels, wind turbines, batteries, electric vehicles. It holds nearly a third of the world's renewable energy patents. If we don't catch up, America will miss the chance to shape the world's climate future in a way that reflects our interests and values, and we'll lose out on countless jobs for the American people."

Biden, like the Europeans, wants to spend big to back the rapid shift to clean energy. US energy secretary Jennifer Granholm underscored the new urgency in Washington when she announced at the summit a US goal to slash the cost of "clean renewable hydrogen" by 80 per cent by 2030, making it competitive with natural gas.

Australia risks being overrun in this clean energy race. If green hydrogen becomes competitive with natural gas by the end of the decade, the oil and gas industry will react by slashing prices, and Australian liquified natural gas prices will plummet. As Forrest put it colourfully in his Boyer lecture, the result will be "like a knife fight in a telephone box".

For now, the Morrison government is making a strategic bet that the energy transformation won't happen this fast. It does not believe that China, let alone India, will be able to radically shift course this decade. This will put the 1.5 Celsius plans out of reach and curb the enthusiasm in developed countries for ambitious targets to cut emissions.

The message from Canberra is that Australia's big exports of liquified natural gas and coal will continue for decades to come.

The latest International Energy Agency review gives some comfort for this view. Energy-related carbon dioxide emissions are on course to surge again in 2021, the second-largest increase in history, reversing most of the pandemic's decline. This year's expected rise in coal use dwarfs that of renewables. Some 80 per cent of the projected growth in coal demand is expected to come from Asia, led by China. As IEA chief Fatih Birol put it, "we remain on a path of dangerous levels of global warming".

Labor's muted response ... has reinforced the view in the government that its current policy is the right course

But the IEA also released its own roadmap in May, warning that if the world wanted to keep to the 1.5 Celsius goal, there could be no new oil and gas fields approved for development beyond 2021, and no new coalmines or mine extensions. The IEA roadmap, "Net Zero by 2050", flew in the face of both Labor and Coalition support for new fossil fuel developments.

Labor's muted response to the Biden summit and the 1.5-degree goal has reinforced the view in the government that its current policy is the right course politically. But outside Australia, there is a growing belief that China's clean energy transition will speed up, due to its capacity for innovation and its need to compete with the United States. Former Australian diplomat Dean Bialek, who is now advising the United Kingdom on preparations for COP26, believes there is a chance that China will bring more to Glasgow than Xi's net zero by 2060 pledge. "I think the Chinese could do it if they wanted. I think their current policy positions are intended to leave a bit of negotiating room this year. Both on the net zero timeline but also in terms of where they can get to by 2030," said Bialek. "And indeed whether they could potentially look at bringing forward the current target on peaking of emissions – which is currently expressed as 'around 2030' – to a much earlier date, to 2025, is one that has been bandied around."

The need for China, India and other big emitters in the developing world to ramp up their ambition in Glasgow explains why the United States and Britain are so exercised about Australia's 2030 target. As a rich developed country with abundant renewable resources, Australia's weak target will give diplomatic succour to other carbon-intensive economies wanting to slow the pace of change, such as Saudi Arabia and Russia.

Boris Johnson invited Morrison to Cornwall for the G7 meeting in June in part because of this. His other special guests were India, South Africa and South Korea. In their final communiqué, the G7 leaders reaffirmed their commitment to reach net zero no later than 2050 and to halve their collective emissions by 2030. They also called for international investment in unabated coal-power generation to stop, committing to end new government support for it by the close of this year.

The message to Morrison from the entire G7 leadership was that big-emitting economies such as Australia needed to bring their highest possible ambition to cut emissions to Glasgow. But Morrison baulked again at the G7, refusing to give either Biden or Johnson a commitment to reach net zero by 2050 or to agree to an ambitious 2030 target. Instead he kicked the decision down the road.

In Canberra, where the climate wars still haunt politicians on both sides, the goal of keeping to 1.5 degrees is still seen by many as the naive aspiration of climate scientists, activists and school strikers. Morrison is certainly trapped in this mentality, quipping to the Business Council dinner this year, "We're not going to achieve net zero in the cafes, dinner parties and wine bars of our inner cities."

Morrison has never accepted the urgency of the science on climate change, but he is increasingly becoming an outlier among world leaders. Between now and November, he has a decision to make: whether he will join those leaders who see the Glasgow summit as the world's last best hope to get the clean energy transition on track – or side with those whose aim is to derail it. ■

RIPPLE EFFECT

The cost of our
Pacific neglect

Wesley Morgan

The first national leader to congratulate Joe Biden on his election as president of the United States was Fiji's prime minister, Frank Baini- marama. There was little doubt what he wanted from the new head of the world's most powerful nation. "Together, we have a planet to save from a climate emergency," he tweeted. Bainimarama knew Pacific island countries had gained a powerful ally in the fight to tackle climate change. Not only would Biden return the United States to the Paris Agreement; he would also, as his administration's list of "immediate priorities" promised, pressure countries "to ramp up the ambition of their climate targets". Bainimarama quickly followed up with a formal letter inviting Biden to attend the 2021 Pacific Islands Forum.

This audacious diplomacy from Fiji fits with a recent pattern from Australia's island neighbours – the fourteen independent nations of the Pacific Islands Forum – who have become adept at working with major powers to shape global diplomacy on climate change. In 2015, for example, Pacific diplomats were instrumental in securing the Paris Agreement, though their role in the negotiations was not widely appreciated in Canberra. Now, Pacific countries are working with some of Australia's closest allies and partners – including the United States and the United Kingdom – to press countries to commit to more ambitious Paris targets before the United Nations Climate Change Conference (COP26) in Glasgow in November 2021.

Australia tends to assume it is the regional leader in the Pacific. On the issue of climate change, however, the tables are turned. Pacific island countries are global leaders, while Australia is isolated from the international consensus.

Australia cannot expect to win friends in the Pacific while promoting fossil fuels and offering to build seawalls. It can be easy to forget, but before the COVID-19 pandemic, prime minister Scott Morrison's signature foreign policy was the "Pacific step-up" – an initiative intended to cement Australia's position as a security partner of choice for Pacific states. But Morrison is learning the hard way that the step-up will not succeed until Australia does more to tackle the issue that Pacific island leaders see as their main security threat: climate change.

Step-down in Tuvalu

Scott Morrison likes to say Australia is part of the Pacific "family", and in many respects he is right. Australia is the most powerful and wealthy member of the Pacific Islands Forum, a valued development partner and a key donor for Pacific regional organisations. Many Pacific islanders have family in Australia, and thousands travel to regional Australian communities each year to pick fruit at harvest time. Australia is also an indispensable ally in times of major disasters. When island communities are devastated by monster cyclones – increasingly a feature of life in the region – they are glad to see Australian naval vessels on the horizon delivering supplies, and military personnel on the ground helping to rebuild villages. But an ambivalence remains. Australia is not really a Pacific country. Connections with, and across, the Pacific Ocean are not central to Australian identity in the same way they are for Pacific island countries. Australians themselves are not sure of their place in the Pacific. When, for example, the Lowy Institute polled people to ask, only 31 per cent of respondents thought Australia was part of the Pacific. With its Polynesian heritage, Aotearoa New Zealand has a greater claim to cultural connection, but Pacific leaders tend to associate Wellington closely with Canberra. The region's two developed countries are referred to as "big brothers", part of the Pacific by geography but set apart by wealth and national identity.

For Australia, engagement with Pacific island countries is driven, above all, by a strategic imperative to maintain political influence and to deny the islands to other powers. In the context of the US alliance, Pacific island states are understood as part of Australia's sphere of influence. Security relations are shaped by the ANZUS Treaty, but also by an ancillary Australia–US naval cooperation agreement – the 1951

Radford-Collins Agreement – which deems Australia responsible for maritime security in the southwest Pacific. This results in a curious state of affairs: Australia views itself as a regional leader, yet its identity as a Pacific nation remains uncertain. To compound matters, Australia's attention span is short, and engagement with the Pacific tends to be episodic, driven by periodic crises that are understood to require Australian intervention, such as the civil war in Bougainville in the 1990s, or coups in Fiji and unrest in Solomon Islands in the early 2000s. Between these crises, Canberra tends to forget the Pacific again.

A new chapter of Australia's episodic attention to the Pacific was written in recent years. Again, perceived security threats were the catalyst, especially the prospect of

"I thought Morrison was a good friend of mine; apparently not"

China leveraging infrastructure loans to establish a military base. In 2018, then prime minister Malcolm Turnbull raised the alarm, explaining "we would view with great concern the establishment of any foreign military bases in those Pacific Island countries and neighbours of ours". Concern about China's growing presence underpinned a new foreign policy initiative – the Pacific step-up – which sought to integrate Pacific states into Australia's economic and security institutions. Initially, Morrison was enthusiastic about the step-up. In his first year as prime minister, he visited Fiji (twice), Solomon Islands, Tuvalu and Vanuatu – a personal investment in the relationship with Pacific island countries unheard of from an Australian prime minister. He was, for the most part, warmly embraced by island leaders. But there was one area where tensions remained high. When Morrison joined the Fijian prime minister for a public dinner in Suva, Bainimarama was blunt: "From where we are sitting," he told Morrison, "we cannot imagine how the interests of any single industry can be placed above the welfare of Pacific peoples [and] vulnerable people the world over." There was no getting past it: Australia was the world's largest coal exporter, and Pacific leaders understood climate change as a direct threat to their security.

At the 2019 Pacific Islands Forum, held in Tuvalu, Morrison met with Pacific leaders in an open-air community hall on the atoll island of Funafuti. As they deliberated, they could see ocean waves pounding the reef out one window, and the calm waters of the lagoon out the other. The threat posed by rising seas can't have been far from anyone's mind. Pacific leaders implored Morrison to support a regional declaration calling for urgent action on climate change. The ailing Tongan prime minister 'Akilisi Pōhiva, who died weeks later, even shed tears. But Morrison ruled out language in the draft declaration that would be difficult for him at home, especially on emissions reduction and phasing out coal. He repeatedly reminded of Australia's financial support to Pacific countries and pointed out that Australia's carbon emissions were dwarfed by China's. Island leaders were incensed. The leaders' retreat became a bruising twelve-hour stand-off that almost broke down altogether. There were calls for Australia to be ousted from the Pacific Islands Forum. Samoa and Fiji suggested China may be a preferable partner. Bainimarama told reporters, "I thought Morrison was a good friend of mine; apparently not ... The Chinese don't insult us. They don't go down and tell the world that we've given this much money to the Pacific islands. They don't do that. They're good people, definitely better than Morrison."

Morrison thought Pacific leaders would welcome the $500 million climate adaptation package he announced in Tuvalu. Yet, before he flew out to the Pacific Islands Forum, his office briefed influential Sydney radio broadcaster Alan Jones to explain none of the funds would be new money. It would instead be diverted, over a number of years, from elsewhere in the aid program. It should have been no surprise that this was not well received. Incredibly, Australian officials were alarmed by how badly things went for Morrison in Tuvalu. They felt he had been ambushed by Pacific leaders. But, as one prominent regional journalist pointed out, it is only an ambush if no one knows it is coming. The signs were all there that Pacific leaders would not be for turning. They had come to understand climate change as a first-order threat, and they wanted Australia – the largest member of the regional "family" – to join their efforts to drive global action. As Tuvalu's prime minister, Enele Sopoaga, explained: "No matter how much money you put on the table,

> **The signs were all there that Pacific leaders would not be for turning**

it doesn't give you the excuse not to do the right thing. Cutting down your emissions, including not opening your coalmines, that is the thing we want to see."

Island diplomacy

Morrison's underestimation of Pacific leaders' resolve reflects a tendency in Canberra to see the Pacific through an Australian lens – as a series of small, isolated states in its backyard, beset with challenges, occasionally serious ones that might impact Australia and require intervention. Not enough attention is paid to the priorities of Pacific states, or to the ways they have independently pursued their own interests. Short on guns and treasure, the island states are often assumed to have no influence in international affairs. But the world is not run only by the powerful, and Pacific island states are not without influence. Together, they are sovereign over a large swathe of the Earth's surface and form an important voting bloc at the United Nations.

In the decades since independence, Pacific island countries have successfully worked together to achieve foreign policy goals, even when opposed by powerful nations. For example, Pacific diplomats took a lead role in negotiations with major powers to secure recognition of their exclusive economic zones under the United Nations Convention on the Law of the Sea. Island countries took on Japan, South Korea and Taiwan to ban driftnet fishing in the South Pacific. In a series of tense negotiations, which included Pacific states impounding US fishing vessels, they reached a deal on a regional treaty governing US boats fishing in their waters. Despite French opposition, island countries successfully lobbied to have both New Caledonia and French Polynesia added to the UN list of non-self-governing territories. At the height of the Cold War, Pacific countries worked with Australia and New Zealand to establish a South Pacific Nuclear Free Zone and pressured France to end nuclear testing in the region. More recently, Pacific states have pursued diplomacy to protect the world's oceans, helping to secure an ocean goal in the UN's Sustainable Development Goals. Fiji has been especially active on the global stage. In recent times it has presided over the United Nations General Assembly (2016), the UN climate talks (2017) and the UN Human Rights Council (2021), and it hosted the inaugural UN Ocean Conference in 2017. Fiji's ambassador to New York, Peter Thomson, is currently the UN Special Envoy for the Ocean.

Australia's "go slow" approach diluted Pacific regional diplomacy

Pacific countries began pursuing collective diplomacy on climate change in the late 1980s, when a scientific consensus on the dangers of global warming emerged. Initially, Australia was in support. At the 1991 Pacific Islands Forum, for example, Canberra backed a declaration that global warming and sea-level rise presented a "great risk to the cultural, economic and physical survival" of Pacific nations. Forum leaders called for urgent action, including a "strong and substantive" global convention that would see immediate reductions in greenhouse gas emissions. From the mid-1990s, however, Australia reassessed its approach. Concerned about the potential economic costs, Australia began to drag its feet in the United Nations climate talks and to minimise its obligations to reduce emissions.

Australia's "go slow" approach diluted Pacific regional diplomacy by denying island countries the chance to use the Pacific Islands Forum to press for shared climate goals. Canberra exercised a veto over regional declarations put forward by Pacific states, including in the lead-ups to the 1997 Kyoto summit, the ill-fated 2009 Copenhagen conference and the 2015 Paris climate talks. Before Copenhagen, for example, Pacific island countries called for a global emissions reduction of 95 per cent by 2050. At that year's Pacific Islands Forum, held in Cairns, Kevin Rudd convinced island leaders to scale back the target to 50 per cent. Ahead of the Paris summit, Pacific leaders made it clear they wanted a treaty to limit warming to 1.5 degrees Celsius above pre-industrial levels. This was a threshold they felt should not be crossed, as doing so would threaten the survival of low-lying atoll countries such as Kiribati, Tuvalu and Marshall Islands. At the 2015 Pacific Islands Forum, however, then prime minister Tony Abbott managed to block any reference to the 1.5 degrees goal. Following that meeting, an angry Kiribati president Anote Tong suggested Australia should leave the forum if Canberra would not back island positions in the global climate talks.

Differences on climate change prompted Pacific island countries to go around Australia and work outside the Pacific Islands Forum to pursue collective diplomacy. Pacific leaders issued their own regional declarations through the Pacific Islands Development Forum, an island-only body established by Fiji, of which neither Australia nor New Zealand is a member. In global negotiations, Pacific countries aggregated common positions through the Pacific Small Island Developing States grouping at the United Nations. Meetings of Pacific ambassadors to New York became important for the development of negotiating positions. Pacific diplomats also worked with counterparts from island countries in the Caribbean and Indian Ocean as part of the Alliance of Small Island States, a significant negotiating coalition in UN climate talks. Some countries, notably Marshall Islands, also collaborated with major powers such as the European Union. Through this independent diplomacy, Pacific island countries have shaped global cooperation on climate change. Indeed, they have had more influence, and played a more important role, than Australia. Perhaps nowhere is this more evident than in the negotiation of the Paris Agreement.

The Paris coup

On 9 December 2015, at an industrial-sized conference centre in the outer-Paris suburb of Le Bourget, Australia's foreign minister, Julie Bishop, sought out her Marshall Islands counterpart, Tony de Brum. Striding through a sea of ministers and officials gathered for COP21, Bishop was determined to have her photo taken with the grey-haired, grandfatherly statesman. She wanted to find him because he had taken her by surprise. The talks, which were in their second week, were progressing slowly. Everyone was worried the summit would be "another

Copenhagen", a reference to the 2009 conference, which had ended in failure, without a global agreement. Much to Bishop's surprise, however, de Brum, representing a Pacific atoll of just over 50,000 people, had emerged in Paris as the leader and spokesperson for a coalition of more than 100 nations, including the European Union and the United States, that was now determined to secure a treaty. Member states of the High Ambition Coalition had been meeting for months, generally in secret, but had waited to break cover, hoping that doing so would seal the deal. With three days of talks left in Paris, de Brum held a press conference announcing that a major bloc of countries was backing an ambitious agreement. At this stage, the Australian minister hadn't heard of the coalition.

It was genius negotiating strategy. In the years leading up to the Paris conference, Marshall Islands had quietly approached countries wanting to achieve a meaningful agreement. Working closely with the European Union, and supported by independent advisers, it stitched together a coalition across the traditional negotiating blocs that had bedevilled previous climate talks. For decades, negotiations had been stalled by arguments between developed and developing countries about who was most responsible for climate change and how much finance would be provided to poorer nations to help deal with its impacts. During 2015, de Brum convened a core group of foreign ministers from both sides, which met at least three times, including once on the sidelines of the UN General Assembly. Worried their email accounts would be hacked, they handwrote their sensitive communications.

They developed a shared goal: a global treaty to set a long-term goal in line with scientific advice, along with a mechanism to review countries' emissions commitments every five years. This mechanism was intended as a ratchet, to force countries to set more ambitious targets over time.

In Paris, it looked like the talks would again stall on the rich–poor split between nations. Issues around finance, legal liability and compensation were especially difficult. There was concern any agreement would lack real ambition. Midway through the talks, on the evening of 6 December, members of the High Ambition Coalition met at a Michelin-starred restaurant for dinner. Among them were diplomats and ministers from Marshall Islands, Tuvalu, Norway, Angola, St Lucia, Grenada, Mexico, Colombia, the European Union and the United States. Over foie gras and oysters, they forged a plan. Two days later, 8 December, the European Union Commissioner for Climate Action and Energy, Miguel Arias Cañete, announced the "African, Caribbean and Pacific" grouping of states would join the coalition, swelling membership to ninety-odd countries. The following day, 9 December, the United States announced it would also join. But the breakthrough came on 11 December, when de Brum met with Brazil's environment minister, Izabella Teixeira, and convinced Brazil to join. Brazil was part of the BASIC grouping – a negotiating coalition of economically powerful countries Brazil, South Africa, India and China. This was a game-changer, ensuring that India and China would not veto the final agreement.

On 12 December, de Brum walked to the final plenary session of the Paris negotiations flanked by Cañete and US Special Envoy for Climate Change Todd Stern. All three wore medallions on their lapels that had been fashioned from coconut leaves by two women from the Marshallese delegation. Canete told the media that "when we walked all together ... I knew that we would get a good deal". At the end of that session, the French foreign minister banged his gavel, signalling the achievement of the first global agreement to tackle the climate crisis. Thousands of delegates applauded. The tears flowed.

Julie Bishop did manage to have her photo taken with de Brum, and she told media in Paris that Australia would join the High Ambition Coalition. But joining required credentials. As de Brum explained, "We are delighted to learn of Australia's interest and look forward to hearing what more they may be able to do to join our coalition." He clearly felt Australia was not bringing enough to the table. When Australia announced its first Paris Agreement target – to reduce emissions by 26 to 28 per cent below 2005 levels by 2030 – de Brum complained that if the rest of the world followed Australia's lead, vulnerable nations such as his would disappear. The following year, when members of the High Ambition Coalition met at a New York signing ceremony for the Paris Agreement, Australia was not invited. The global leadership of Pacific island countries was instead being recognised. When US president Barack Obama met island leaders in Hawaii in September 2016, he explained: "We could not have gotten a Paris Agreement without the incredible efforts and hard work of the island nations ... they made an enormous difference."

After decades of incremental negotiations, the Paris Agreement was a major diplomatic achievement. But it was not a set-and-forget agreement. Instead, it provided a framework for states to work together to achieve the mammoth task of decarbonising the global economy by the middle of this century. Under the agreement, countries are required to set more ambitious targets every five years. Which is why this year's climate conference in Glasgow is no ordinary summit. Coming five years after the Paris Agreement (with a one-year delay due to the COVID-19 pandemic), COP26 is a stress-test of global cooperation to tackle the climate crisis. Expectations are high that countries will bring new targets and commit to achieving net-zero emissions by 2050.

Unlike Australia, other countries have leveraged climate policy to win friends in the region

So far, the signs are good. In the past year alone, the United States, the European Union, the United Kingdom, Japan, South Korea and Canada have all announced plans to achieve net-zero emissions by 2050. China – the world's largest emitter – has set a 2060 target. Collectively, these pledges send a powerful signal that the world is starting to take climate change seriously, and the markets are listening. Major finance houses are divesting from fossil fuels. Hundreds of corporations have put net-zero emissions targets in place. There is hope yet that we might stabilise the Earth's climate system and avoid the worst impacts of global heating. A remarkable but little understood aspect of this shift toward post-carbon economies is that it might not have come about were it not for the creative and determined diplomacy of Pacific island states. Sometimes, the global system pivots on the actions of its smallest members.

A new Pacific step-up

In the six years since the Paris conference, geostrategic competition between the United States and China has prompted major powers to take a renewed interest in Pacific island states. China, through its Belt and Road Initiative, has financed important infrastructure projects in the region, including wharves, airports and roads. The United States has responded with hundreds of millions of dollars in aid as part of a 2019 "Pacific Pledge". Japan too has committed new funds for infrastructure, while New Zealand bumped up aid as part of a 2018 "Pacific Reset". The United Kingdom has dived back into the region with a 2019 "Pacific Uplift" that includes three new diplomatic posts in the Pacific. French president Emmanuel Macron visited Australia and New Caledonia in 2018 to remind everyone that France was a "Pacific power" with a keen interest in making sure China does not dominate the region. Even Indonesia announced a "Pacific Elevation" in 2019. Amid these pledges, resets, elevations and uplifts, Australia's Pacific step-up is in a crowded field.

Unlike Australia, however, other countries have leveraged climate policy to win friends in the region. They have highlighted steps they are taking to reduce emissions and have promoted Pacific leadership on climate. France, for example, has recast its Pacific image from a colonial power that tests nuclear bombs to a key partner in the climate fight.

At the 2015 Paris conference, then French president François Hollande told island leaders that "France is fully a country of the Pacific ... we share the life and future of the big Pacific family". The following year, the French territories New Caledonia and French Polynesia were welcomed as members of the Pacific Islands Forum.

As other powers have exercised climate diplomacy they have, perhaps inadvertently, highlighted Australia's lack of climate action. In 2018, New Zealand legislated a net-zero emissions target for 2050, which in the eyes of Pacific leaders set Wellington apart from Canberra. At the 2019 Pacific Islands Forum leaders' retreat, while Morrison argued over the text of a regional climate declaration, Bainimarama took a lunchtime walk with Jacinda Ardern.

While Pacific countries understand the climate crisis as an urgent threat, Australia does not

He live-tweeted a picture of the two strolling the Funafuti foreshore, captioning it, "When combatting climate change, it's good to have an ally like New Zealand in your corner. Together, we can save Tuvalu, the Pacific, and the world. Vinaka vakalevu [thank you so much] for the passion you bring to this fight, @jacindaardern". Ardern told reporters that "Australia has to answer to the Pacific" on climate change. The contrast between other countries and Australia is especially pronounced this year, as major powers the United States, the European Union and the United Kingdom work with Pacific island countries to press for stronger targets before the COP26 summit.

While Pacific countries understand the climate crisis as an urgent threat to their security, Australia does not yet see it in the same way. This has led to a mismatch in strategic priorities. Australia's Pacific step-up is driven by security concerns, particularly that China could leverage infrastructure lending to establish a military base in the Pacific. But island leaders take a different view. At the 2018 Pacific Islands Forum, they issued a declaration formally reaffirming climate change as the "single greatest threat to the livelihoods, security and wellbeing of the peoples of the Pacific". Compared with a more coercive China, and competition between the United States and China, island leaders see the impacts of climate change – stronger cyclones, devastating floods, rising seas, dying reefs and ocean acidification – as more tangible and immediate threats. As Fiji's military commander, Rear Admiral Viliame Naupoto, told the 2019 Shangri-La Security Dialogue in Singapore:

> I believe there are three major powers in competition in our region. There is the US … there is China [and] the third competitor is climate change. Of the three, climate change is winning, and climate change exerts the most influence on countries in our part of the world. If there is any competition, it is with climate change.

Increasingly, the rest of the world shares the Pacific's perception. Australia is out of step not only with Pacific island states, but also with major powers and friends. UK prime minister Boris Johnson told the

UN Security Council in February 2021 that "it is absolutely clear that climate change is a threat to our collective security and the security of our nations". US Special Presidential Envoy for Climate John Kerry said failing to address the climate crisis was like "marching forward to what is almost tantamount to a mutual suicide pact". US president Joe Biden has said that "if we don't get this right, nothing else will matter". The United States, like Pacific island countries, wants Canberra to do more to reduce emissions, and to move away from coal-fired power. It is in Australia's interests to act, because the climate crisis is a critical security threat to Australia as well. The bushfires of early 2020 – which killed dozens of people, incinerated millions of animals, turned the sky blood-red and rendered the air in Australian cities a health hazard – were a warning. They were a window to the catastrophic future Australia faces if the world fails to take urgent action to reduce emissions.

For Australia, the costs of inaction on climate far outweigh the costs of action. Indeed, failure to plan for the inevitable transition would not only be a missed opportunity to tackle the climate emergency, but also a missed economic boom. Australia is well placed to take advantage of surging demand for renewable energy, and for alternatives to emissions-intensive products. There is no doubt change is needed.

A new Australian climate policy would allow a reset of Australia's Pacific strategy. Morrison himself understands how important climate action is for Australia's relationships in the region. Soon after he became prime minister, he was asked by Alan Jones why we shouldn't just "rip up" the Paris Agreement and bow out of it. His response was telling.

He told Jones the agreement was "enormously important" to Australia's island neighbours, "who are strategic partners in the Pacific". He was right, of course. Good relationships with Pacific island countries are vitally important for Australian security. If Australia begins to shift its approach to climate change, it will have a chance to work with Pacific countries as climate partners. The first order of business will be to announce a target of net-zero emissions by 2050. Doing so at this year's Pacific Islands Forum would tell the world Australia is committed to action and working with Pacific island countries to achieve it.

Canberra also needs to set a new target to reduce emissions over the next decade. Australia's 2030 target is both out of date and woefully inadequate. A more ambitious climate policy would help cement Australia's place as a security partner of choice for Pacific countries. As Bainimarama – the incoming chair of the Pacific Islands Forum – has said, "strong commitments will make strong friendships". Working through the Pacific Islands Forum to pursue climate diplomacy would strengthen Australia's credentials as a regional power and do much to enhance its image on the global stage. But Canberra must embrace the opportunity while it still can. After decades of trying to sabotage Pacific climate diplomacy, Australia can only hope it will still be welcomed into the Pacific family. ■

DOUBLE GAME

How Australian diplomacy protects fossil fuels

Richard Denniss and Allan Behm

In recent decades, just as the world began to commit to reducing carbon emissions, Australia has invested in an enormous expansion of its fossil fuel production and exports. Domestic coal production has more than doubled since the early 1990s, with export volumes growing by the same amount – Australia produced approximately 571 million tonnes of coal in 2017–18, exporting around 75 per cent of it, up from 55 per cent in 1990–91. And its gas exports have increased tenfold, from around 7 million tonnes to 75 million tonnes. Australia is now the third-largest fossil fuel exporter in the world, behind Saudi Arabia and Russia.

Despite the significant financial, environmental and political cost of building new coalmines and oil wells on farmland and in pristine environments, and continuing to allow offshore oil exploration within sight of large population centres, successive Australian governments have committed not just to facilitating increases in fossil fuel exports, but also to subsidising them. The conservative National Party, which has traditionally claimed to support agricultural communities, has begun to prioritise coalmines and gas wells over agricultural land use. In 2019, when *The Project* host Waleed Aly asked the deputy prime minister, Nationals party leader Michael McCormack, if he could name a single policy area where his party had sided with the interests of farmers over those of the mining industry, he responded, "Not straight off the top of my head."

In the words of the then federal resources minister, Senator Matt Canavan: "The development of almost every minerals province in Australia has involved government investment."

Clearly, Australia has no plans to transition away from fossil fuels. It is in the middle of an enormous, decades-long project to increase its production and export of iron ore, coal and gas. Not surprisingly, successive Australian governments have geared Australia's foreign policy to facilitate these exports. For decades, Australia has consistently undermined global efforts to reduce greenhouse gas emissions. It has even prioritised support for its resources sector over its relationships with its Pacific neighbours, jeopardising its efforts to contain China's influence in the Pacific. In short, increasing the export of fossil fuels has been a key objective of Australian foreign policy.

Leader among laggards

The Biden administration's recent reset of US climate policy has reshaped the ambitions of a large number of countries. In April 2021, US secretary of state Antony Blinken made a not-so-veiled threat: "When countries continue to rely on coal for a significant amount of their energy, or invest in new coal factories, or allow for massive deforestation, they will hear from the United States and our partners about how harmful these actions are."

But US and international shifts in climate policy have, to date, had no impact on Australia. This is perhaps unsurprising. Australia has always been a laggard in global climate negotiations. While Australia is the permanent chair of the Umbrella Group of countries, a key negotiating body of signatories to the United Nations Framework Convention on Climate Change (UNFCCC), it was alone in its insistence on the right to rely on so-called "carryover credits" from the Kyoto commitment period – a position that a former German climate change negotiator, Malte Meinshausen, described as a "betrayal of trust".

Since the 2015 United Nations Climate Change Conference (COP21) in Paris, Australia has also helped developing countries to build a moral and economic case to increase their fossil fuel emissions. In an article titled "The World Needs More Australian Coal, Not Less", Senator Canavan stated, "Australia's resources have played such an important role in helping build a better world that we must continue to expand their production and use, and we will continue to reduce the world's emissions as we do." Further, Australia has actively lobbied against restrictions on developing countries building or financing new coal-fired power stations, and lobbied developing countries in South-East Asia to buy more Australian coal. Departmental briefing notes prepared for Canavan include the assertion that "with a significant expansion of coal-fired power in Bangladesh expected in the near future, there are opportunities to establish a new export market for thermal coal". Briefing notes prepared for Prime Minister Scott Morrison in 2019, prior to his official visit to Vietnam, stated that coal exports to Vietnam could "partially mitigate declining exports elsewhere, notably China" and recommended "a focus on coal exports … as part of the Prime Minister's planned visit".

Lest there be any doubt as to Australia's foreign policy ambitions, Morrison declared in 2017, two years after the COP21, that "Australia's national interest demands that coal continue to be part of our future energy equation, not just here in Australia, but around the world".

Australia's determination to rebuke allies such as the United States and the United Kingdom on emissions-reduction targets is not without diplomatic cost. It's important, therefore, to consider what might be gained. Australia appears to be seeking to position itself as a "leader among the laggards" in order to maximise its fossil fuel exports and the period of time those exports can be maintained. Australia has presumably assessed that the economic and domestic political benefits from increased coal and gas exports exceed the likely diplomatic and trade costs (such as the effect on efforts to sign a free trade agreement with the United Kingdom). By resisting committing to net zero and to a rapid phase-out of coal, Australia helps enable developing countries to continue to invest in new coal-fired power stations and to purchase Australian coal exports.

Scott Morrison has repeatedly claimed that Australia is "leading the world" on investment in renewable technology. Yet Australia's emissions from electricity generation, transport, industry and chemical processes are increasing, while most other OECD countries have transformed their energy systems and reduced emissions. In April, Morrison told the Business Council of Australia that the nation is "leading the way" on climate, while talking down the achievements of trading partners such as Japan and the United States in reducing their emissions. In an address to world leaders at President Biden's Leaders Summit on Climate, he said that Australia is doing "more than most other similar economies". Yet when emissions reductions from land use, land use change and the forestry sector are excluded, Australia's emissions are rising, when those of nearly every other developed country have been falling.

Australia is often accused of failing to understand the threats and opportunities associated with climate change. In fact, the opposite is true. Australia is the fourteenth-largest economy in the world. It is in the Five Eyes intelligence alliance, the OECD and the G20; has an annual expenditure on foreign affairs and diplomacy of $6.1 billion; and is often perceived as "punching above its weight" on foreign policy. Australia understands the potential threat to one of its largest export industries. Its foreign policy apparatus has been deployed, for decades, to protect that industry from global efforts to tackle climate change. To date, it has been extremely successful.

Fossil fuel acceleration

The scale of Australia's fossil fuel extraction is hard to comprehend. Its share of the world's export coal market is larger than Saudi Arabia's share of the world oil market, yet new coalmines with the ability to nearly double that capacity have already been approved or are seeking approval. In New South Wales, there are currently twenty-three new coalmines and mine expansions seeking approval. Former Australian prime minister Malcolm Turnbull recently stated that coalmine approvals were "out of control" and called for a moratorium on approving new mines. He was subsequently sacked by the New South Wales state government from a government climate change advisory board.

Australia's expansion of gas production and exports has been similarly ambitious. At the time of the COP21, Australia had no capacity to export liquified natural gas (LNG) from its east coast. But after $60 billion of investment in liquefaction and export facilities in Gladstone, Queensland, Australia rapidly went on to export more LNG than any other nation, surpassing Qatar in 2019. The Morrison government remains determined to exploit enormous new gas basins and is pressuring state governments that have sought to limit new gas developments. According to the Australian National Resources Statement, a long-term blueprint for the sector released in 2019: "The Beetaloo Sub-basin in the Northern Territory is a world-class shale gas resource … While the scale of the gas resources in the Beetaloo Sub-basin is vast, exploration is only just getting underway." And then there's the Canning Basin in Western Australia, which has "significant potential for new gas and oil discoveries": "The Canning Basin is home to 90 per cent of Australia's prospective shale gas, 40 per cent of prospective tight gas and over 80 per cent of prospective shale oil. Despite an upswing in exploration since 2010, the Canning Basin is still considered under-explored."

While many countries have sought to phase out subsidies to the fossil fuel industry, the Morrison government used the COVID-19-induced recession to advocate a "gas led recovery". It proposed more public funding to support new gas projects. The Australian government provides subsidies and tax concessions to fossil fuel producers and does not rely heavily on tax revenue from the sector. For example, Australia exports more LNG than Qatar yet collects less than one-fiftieth of the tax it does. According

While the world has been talking about reducing emissions, Australia has been investing in fossil fuel

to the Australian Taxation Office, Chevron and Exxon Mobil paid no tax on $15 billion of combined revenues in 2018. It is not clear why successive state and federal governments have subsidised the fossil fuel industry despite collecting relatively small amounts of revenue. One explanation is governments' focus on the jobs associated with the construction of major projects rather than the lasting economic benefits.

Other countries, such as Germany, have debated how best to help coalmining regions transition away from reliance on fossil fuels. Yet Australian state and federal governments are working to open up new areas, such as the Galilee Basin, to coal dependence. The Galilee Basin, located in Far North Queensland, is around 1000 kilometres away from any existing coalmines.

Similarly, while countries such as New Zealand and Denmark have announced forms of moratoria on new exploration for oil, the Australian government not only has continued to subsidise new oil and gas exploration, but also threatened to withhold funding to the Victorian state government unless it lifted a moratorium it had imposed on gas fracking.

In short, while the world has been talking about reducing greenhouse gas emissions, Australia has been investing in, and planning for, significant growth in fossil fuel production and exports. As the current federal resources minister, Keith Pitt, recently exclaimed:

Coal sales to Vietnam and India were stronger, reaffirming the competitiveness of Australian coal, and its reputation for high quality in global markets. This again reinforces the importance of coal as an Australian export commodity and that it will remain so for many more years to come … The result is a great testament to the work of our resources industry to maintain full operations throughout 2020 as the coronavirus pandemic wreaked havoc on many other industry sectors across the world.

Australia's diplomatic prowess

The effective halving of Australia's foreign affairs budget over the past two decades might suggest that it has cut its losses in the business of international diplomacy – an admission of defeat. History, however, tells the opposite story. Australia is very good at diplomacy, especially when the government sets clear objectives, provides sufficient resources and deploys competent negotiators.

Australia's diplomatic history boasts many bilateral highlights: maintaining diplomatic representation in Jakarta while Australian and Indonesian forces were exchanging fire during Konfrontasi (1963–66); establishing a critically important relationship with China in 1972; building a deep strategic partnership with Japan; and expanding the relationship with the United States beyond the ANZUS Treaty and its intelligence partnership to include a multi-faceted free trade agreement.

Australia has the capacity to change the speed of international policymaking

But Australia's greatest diplomatic achievements are in multilateralism. The 1961 Antarctic Treaty was a spectacular negotiating success initiated by the first Menzies government. It demilitarised and denuclearised a continent and demonstrated that cooperation between suspicious superpowers during the Cold War was possible. The Cairns Group, set up by trade minister John Dawkins in 1984, forced the inclusion of agriculture – particularly the vexed question of subsidies – in global trade negotiations. And, during the global financial crisis of 2008, the Rudd government led a major diplomatic effort to persuade the United States, and President George W. Bush in particular, to convene a global leaders' meeting of the G20 in Washington. At a subsequent meeting in 2009, Australia led the G20 leaders to designate it "the premier forum for ... international economic co-operation". This diplomatic success reformed the global economic architecture, and secured a continuing place for Australia at the table.

Australia's impressive diplomatic record demonstrates that it has the capacity, if it wants, to change the speed, if not the direction, of international policymaking. And Australia has drawn on these skills in seeking to shape global climate policy. It has fought hard to protect its ability to export fossil fuels in a wide range of forums over a long period of time.

How Australia undermines global climate action

Successive Australian governments have been adamant that they accept the science of climate change and the need to reduce greenhouse gas emissions. Australian representatives even voiced their frustration at being excluded from the High Ambition Coalition formed at the COP21. But Australia's actions in a wide range of multilateral forums, combined with the shape and size of Australia's domestic energy investment, suggest that it has other motives.

The whole structure of the UNFCCC framework helps fossil fuel exporters such as Australia by focusing attention on countries that burn fossil fuels, not on the countries that produce them. For example, Australia is the world's largest exporter of iron ore and the second-largest exporter of coal, but when China combines Australian iron ore and coal to make steel for cars that are exported back to Australia, China is assigned responsibility for the emissions from steel-making and car manufacture. Further, the UNFCCC framework has made achieving emissions reduction targets even easier for countries that "offshore" much of their emissions-intensive manufacturing, as Australia has done in recent decades. Neither the Paris Agreement nor the Kyoto Protocol mentions the words "coal" or "gas".

Arguably, Australia has been undermining both the significance and the effectiveness of global efforts to tackle climate change from the very beginning. In 1992, the United Nations hosted the Earth Summit, at which 117 world leaders – including US president George H.W. Bush – negotiated the UNFCCC. Australia chose not to send its prime minister, Paul Keating, and instead sent its environment minister, Ros Kelly. Minutes of the relevant cabinet meeting note that Australia "is a major user and exporter of greenhouse gas producing fossil fuels and energy intensive products; it could be significantly affected by global environmental change" and that "a decision by Australia not to sign the Convention would be criticised by domestic environment interests and could also attract international criticism, particularly in the Pacific region". It goes on to reassure Cabinet that:

> Parties are obliged to take into consideration the situation of Parties with economies that are highly dependent on the production, processing, export and use of fossil fuels. These two provisions will give relevant countries, including Australia, flexibility in fulfilling their obligations under the Convention.

The subsequent Coalition government of John Howard was ultimately responsible for Australia's negotiating position at Kyoto, where Australia infamously threatened to walk out of the meeting unless the so-called "Australia clause" – which allowed a broad definition of land-use emissions to be included in the total calculation of greenhouse gas emissions – was included. This clause delivered enormous benefits to Australia, which sought to maintain the appearance of climate action while planning a large expansion of its coal and gas exports.

Despite already benefiting from a sympathetic accounting regime, Australia, one of the highest emitters per capita, has since sought, and obtained, some of the least ambitious emission targets of any OECD country. But perhaps the clearest evidence that Australia's foreign policy is geared towards slowing the global reduction of fossil fuel use is the breadth of diplomatic forums in which Australia has fought against climate action.

For example, in 2010, Australia signed on to the G20 commitment to phase out fossil fuel subsidies. Then, it reported to the G20 that, because it had no such subsidies in place, it had nothing to phase out. Documents subsequently obtained under freedom of information laws showed that several Australian government departments had initially identified seventeen fossil fuel subsidies that would need to be removed, but this advice was ignored when crafting the response to the G20.

Australia's hosting of a G20 meeting in 2014 provides an even starker example of this determination to slow diplomatic consensus around the need to lower greenhouse gas emissions. The then

Australian prime minister, Tony Abbott, refused to "clutter up" the agenda of the G20 meeting with talk of emissions; instead, he opened the summit with a speech celebrating his success in removing the carbon price introduced by the previous Labor government. In response, President Obama criticised the oft-cited Australian argument that increased coal exports were necessary to alleviate global poverty.

Similarly, as many countries sought to create momentum for change in the lead-up to the Paris Agreement in 2015, Australia was the last of the OECD countries to agree to reduce state aid for the construction of coal-fired power stations in developing countries. While Australia ultimately signed the agreement, it succeeded in introducing multiple exemptions, such as an exception for power stations equipped with carbon capture and storage systems.

Why is Australia so determined not to join international efforts to set short-term targets?

Likewise, in 2016 Australia used its membership of the Asian Infrastructure Investment Bank (AIIB) to lobby against a focus on investments in renewable energy and instead put more emphasis on loans for coal and nuclear power stations. When this lobbying succeeded, Morrison stated:

Australia's national interest demands that coal continue to be part of our future energy equation, not just here in Australia, but around the world. That is why following our strong representations, I am pleased that the AIIB has now put fossil-fuel generation investments back into the mix for their energy sector strategy, which is now under discussion.

More recently, in 2019 Australia stopped making contributions to the global Green Climate Fund, one of the commitments it made just prior to the COP20. The decision came after Morrison's earlier declaration to Alan Jones on breakfast radio that "I'm not going to spend money on global climate conferences and all that sort of nonsense." That same year, Australia gained the distinction of being the last country to rule out the use of "carryover credits" to meet its obligations under the Paris Agreement.

Australia enjoys considerable international power, and the quality of its diplomacy is second to none – when we want it to be. In recent years, the task for Australian diplomats has been clear – to invest time, resources and diplomatic capital in slowing the rate at which global climate action harms Australia's fossil fuel exports.

Why Morrison won't commit to net zero

Each of Australia's eight states and territories has committed to reduce its emissions to net zero by 2050 or before. Yet the Morrison government seems determined to ensure it attracts criticism for failing to commit to achieving what Australia has, in effect, already committed to.

The United Kingdom and the United States have urged Australia to be more ambitious and been vocal in their frustration. For example, in December 2020 they hosted the Climate Ambition Summit to mark the fifth anniversary of the Paris Agreement, and requested signatories to the agreement attend and announce strengthened commitments. Although he pronounced to the Australian parliament that he intended to attend and "correct mistruths" about Australia's lack of ambition, Morrison was blocked from presenting at the summit after he failed to commit to strengthening Australia's commitment to emissions reduction.

Similarly, the European Union has made clear that if Australia does not commit to more ambitious targets, its (non-fossil-fuel) exports to Europe may be met with a carbon tax at the EU border.

Why is the Australian government so determined to only commit to long-term goals, such as net zero with no timetable, and not join international efforts to set short-term targets? Some members of the Morrison government, including Michael McCormack, have repudiated the need for a target of net zero by 2050 on the basis that the future is a long way off: "I'm certainly not worried about what might happen in 30 years' time." This view is shared by former deputy prime minister Barnaby Joyce, who said that "quite a high proportion of us will have passed away ... that's the only thing certain about 2050". Such populist rhetoric is nothing more than a smokescreen for a far-sighted strategy to maximise fossil fuel exports.

If the Australian government genuinely felt that substantial action was not needed now to address future threats, then it would not engage in military procurement, or spend billions of dollars to deliver a new space command within the Australian Defence Force. Nor would it subsidise fossil fuel exploration that takes decades to deliver a final product.

Another possible explanation is the prime minister's frequent assertion that he does not like to make commitments unless he has a plan for achieving them. But there has been no such reluctance by his government, or previous governments, to set targets for outcomes as diverse as public debt, the budget deficit, the rate of vaccination against COVID-19 or international school performance measures. In 2014, then treasurer Joe Hockey lauded his own role in persuading the G20 to commit to boost their collective gross domestic product by US$2 trillion dollars (a target that was not met).

Morrison told the Business Council of Australia's annual dinner:

You won't get emissions down in large developing countries through arbitrary target setting. Quite rightly, they're getting people out of poverty. The pathway to making meaningful impacts on global emissions reductions with these countries is through partnering with them on technological development, making it scalable, making it commercial, making it achievable.

The prime minister's dismissive attitude to the decades-long global UNFCCC process may seem surprising. But his contempt is more easily interpreted when read in conjunction with his claim in the same speech that:

> You will also not reduce the number of coal-fired stations in the world today by forcing the shutdown of Australian coalmines and Australian jobs that go with them. Other countries will just buy the coal from somewhere else, often poorer quality with greater environmental and climate impacts.

Australia is not planning for a world in which the consumption of fossil fuels falls rapidly in the coming decades. It still argues that developing countries need to burn coal to escape poverty, that the burning of more coal is inevitable, and that if such coal is to be burned, it might as well come from Australia. As Senator Canavan put it: "It is good that Australia becomes more prosperous from the sale of coal. We do so because that sale creates value in another country. If you value the reduction of poverty and the economic development of poorer nations, the greater use of coal is good."

Exposing Australia's double game

Australia is not transitioning away from fossil fuels; nor is it bracing for the economic impacts of a worldwide reduction in demand for its coal and gas. On the contrary: Australia is increasing its supply of fossil fuels domestically and, on the international front, is using the full range of diplomatic opportunities available to slow global commitments to net zero. Australia's stated ambition is to increase coal exports to developing countries in South-East Asia. It is therefore clearly in Australia's perceived national interest to reduce the ambition of emissions-reduction pledges made by those countries.

Australia's domestic policy of increasing coal supply at a time of shrinking world demand will result in cheaper prices, and in turn lower the operating costs for foreign coal-fired power stations. Similarly, Australia's foreign policy of protecting subsidies for the construction of new coal-fired power stations helps to lock in new long-term sources of demand for its coal.

Australia wants developing countries to delay efforts to reach their own net-zero targets, so it makes perfect sense for Australia to refuse to make this commitment itself. The diplomatic criticism Australia attracts for its laggard status helps to shield developing countries from that criticism and, in turn, slows the rate at which they might feel compelled to make such commitments.

Australia has succeeded in ensuring that global efforts to reduce greenhouse gas emissions over the past thirty years have not significantly impeded its expansion of fossil fuel exports, and the current pipeline of new fossil fuel projects suggests it expects that success to continue. There are, however, two new factors that have made Australia's strategy harder to implement.

The first is a shift among climate change campaigners, away from a singular focus on emissions reduction targets and towards the supply side of the equation. The UNFCCC process, with its spotlight on commitments by the consumers of fossil fuels, suited countries such as Australia. But campaigns against the Keystone XL pipeline in the United States, oil production from tar sands in Canada and the Adani coalmine in Australia have all highlighted the absurdity of energy-producing countries making commitments to reduce emissions while significantly expanding their extraction of fossil fuels. Calls for action on the supply side, and for governments to implement policies such as moratoria on fossil fuel expansion, have disrupted the "diplomacy as usual" that has concealed Australia's goals and tactics for decades.

Australia can indeed influence international climate policy

The second is that Australia has flatly rejected calls by Pacific island nations to stop building new coalmines. While such a position is consistent with increasing coal exports, it diminishes Australia's standing in the Pacific and boosts the relative status of countries such as New Zealand and Fiji, which vie with Australia for diplomatic leadership in the South Pacific and have supported such "supply-side" commitments. Similarly, Australia's visible support for fossil fuel expansionism gives those countries and blocs that are not planning to boost their fossil fuel exports, such as the European Union, a simple way to isolate Australia beyond the UNFCCC process, which has provided Australia so much diplomatic cover for so long.

For more than a decade, domestic politics in Australia have revolved around the question of whether to introduce a price on carbon.

Ironically, one of the strongest arguments used by the fossil fuel lobby is that any Australian emissions reduction will be insignificant in global terms. Yet the supporters of the fossil fuel industry have shown that Australia can indeed influence international climate policy – they have been using the full range of foreign policy levers to significantly reduce global commitments to cut emissions even before the UNFCCC process began.

It's not yet clear if Australia can continue expanding fossil fuel exports while the world tries to reduce emissions. But what is clear is that state and federal governments in Australia are still subsidising and approving new gas and coal projects. Unless countries that want to drive rapid global emissions reductions create new frameworks to expose Australia's double game, it seems likely that Australia will continue using foreign policy to support its fossil fuel sector. If Prime Minister Morrison is to be taken at his word, the longer it takes developing countries to commit to ambitious emissions-reduction targets, the better it is for Australia. ∎

TOWARDS GLASGOW

Why Australia's climate policy is risking our future

Amanda McKenzie

Fresh from his election win in November 2007, Prime Minister Kevin Rudd addressed the United Nations Climate Change Conference in Bali (COP13). His first act of government had been to sign the formal documents to ratify the Kyoto Protocol, and he told world leaders that Australia "stands ready to assume its responsibility in responding to this challenge". He received rapturous applause and a standing ovation. Rachmat Witoelar, president of the COP13, summed up the feeling in the room: "I think I can speak for all present here by expressing a sigh of relief."

Australia's role in the protocol had always been vexed. The Howard government drove a hard bargain in the 1997 negotiations. First, it demanded that Australia should increase our carbon emissions, while the rest of the industrialised world agreed to decrease theirs. Second, it managed to sneak in a last-minute change to the agreement allowing land clearing to be included in the calculation of a nation's greenhouse-gas emissions, now infamously called the "Australia clause". Countries had agreed that 1990 levels would be the baseline against which they would reduce emissions. This happened to be a year of huge land clearing in Australia, so its inclusion would make meeting the Protocol obligations far easier. John Howard's government left the negotiations with a huge free kick: they could say they were part of global efforts, while increasing emissions by 8 per cent off a baseline year that was already unusually high. Then, as a further affront to international diplomacy, Howard later refused to ratify the agreement, following the lead of the Bush administration.

Rudd's heartfelt speech in Indonesia felt a world away from the cunning, underhanded tactics of a decade earlier. As a conference delegate, I remember feeling full of pride that our nation would finally show some gumption. Reuters described Australia's actions as a highlight.

But why did the world care if Australia was part of the agreement? We have heard the line a million times that Australia pollutes so little we are largely irrelevant to international action. In Bali, the international community didn't seem to think so.

The truth is Australia has always had an important role in the climate story – because of the sheer scale of the pollution we create at home and the amount we export to the world. We are the fifty-fifth-largest country by population, but the fifteenth-largest polluter of carbon dioxide. That means 180 countries pollute less than we do, and puts us firmly within the top twenty climate-polluting countries. We are the largest exporter of liquified gas in the world (having overtaken Qatar in 2019) and the second-largest exporter of thermal coal – two fossil fuels that contribute enormously to climate change. On the flipside, we are a wealthy country with an abundance of renewable energy sources, with significant opportunities to benefit from a clean energy revolution. However, Australia has prioritised protecting fossil fuel interests over safeguarding our citizens from the ravages of climate change. We have become notorious for our weak targets and blocking tactics in global climate conferences and for legitimising problematic US positions during the Bush and Trump administrations.

This was why the spontaneous applause in Bali represented relief, rather than celebration. At home and abroad, it was hoped that Rudd would herald a new era of climate action in Australia that would help build global momentum. Of course, history has played out very differently.

The world has not waited for Australia. In the intervening thirteen years, there has been significant political and economic change worldwide that is accelerating the drive to decarbonisation. There has also been a quiet revolution domestically, driven by the states, business and local government. Whereas in 2007 a handful of homes had solar panels, today there are more than 2.5 million, driven by local and state policy, and plummeting costs. But the lack of federal leadership has exposed Australia to increased security and economic risks. Climate change is accelerating and the consequences – from catastrophic megafires to mass bleaching on the Great Barrier Reef – are now all around us. Our national government's failure to introduce effective national policies means that we are a major contributor to the crisis, and we are missing out on the huge opportunities arising from the global clean energy revolution. Australia's current pollution reduction targets would still have us polluting just slightly less in 2030 than that 1990 baseline set decades ago. However, the next global climate meeting in Glasgow in November offers an opportunity for Australia to reposition itself to contribute positively to the climate crisis and benefit from our natural advantages in clean energy.

Growing security and economic threats

Back in 2007, climate change was generally described as a threat that would affect "our children and grandchildren". Fourteen years later, the children of 2007 have grown up and have now experienced many of the consequences that seemed distant then.

In early 2019, a group of thirty-four former fire and emergency chiefs, led by former NSW fire chief Greg Mullins, warned federal and state governments of the escalating risks of worsening bushfire conditions due to climate change. They were extremely concerned about the approaching fire season and believed that we were not adequately prepared. By winter, fires were already burning, and twenty-one local government areas in New South Wales commenced their Bush Fire Danger Period, months earlier than the usual October start. By September, a number of locations in New South Wales declared "catastrophic conditions", a rating introduced after Black Saturday to indicate conditions that cannot be fought safely. Mullins warned that the summer was going to be the worst he had seen in almost fifty years of fighting fires, and sadly, he was proven right. By March we had experienced simultaneous massive disasters. Communities were razed, thirty-three people died, billions of animals perished, and our firefighters were pushed to their limit.

While people in rural and regional areas felt the worst effects, 80 per cent of Australians experienced the choking smoke, often for weeks on end. I recall waking up and tasting ash in my mouth and assuming there must be a bushfire burning on the edge of Melbourne. The massive inferno was in fact hundreds of kilometres away, devastating Gippsland. What scientists

Australia must prepare for this new era of megafires, intensifying droughts and floods

had predicted decades before was here, and not just on our television screens, but in the very air we were breathing.

The federal government was repeatedly criticised for being ill prepared and flat-footed, having failed to heed the warnings of the fire chiefs and appropriately prepare and resource the response. The dire conditions in early January saw the federal government finally step up its response, compulsorily calling out Australian Defence Force reservists to respond to a disaster on home soil. Over the summer, more than 6500 personnel provided support in the field, sea and air; navy vessels were deployed to evacuate citizens and bring emergency supplies. Our forces were bolstered by defence personnel and fire-fighters from New Zealand, Indonesia, the United States and Japan, among others.

Black Summer – Australia's worst-ever disaster – offers a clear example of the wide-ranging threat from climate change. The economic costs of the fires were enormous and will persist in many regions for years. AMP chief economist Shane Oliver estimated the cost at $20 billion, more than four times 2009's Black Saturday. The disruption to work, shopping and transport was estimated at $12 million to $50 million per day in Sydney alone, while the health costs were estimated at $2 billion. The economic impact will play out over the longer term. For instance, large areas of the Blue Mountains National Park were burnt, inevitably affecting tourism for years to come.

Disasters – fire, flood, drought, coastal inundation, heatwaves – are all becoming more forceful and frequent, and they are happening simultaneously in different parts of Australia. During Black Summer, multiple states and territories experienced extreme danger periods and major disasters at the same time, stretching our ability to respond. Fire seasons across Australia used to be staggered, enabling a sharing of equipment and personnel between states. Similarly, resource sharing with the United States and Canada, from whom we lease many of our aircraft, has become more precarious as our fire seasons increasingly overlap. The number of defence personnel responding to Black Summer was about four times larger than at the height of our involvement in Afghanistan. As defence force chief Angus Campbell stated in

September 2019, "Deploying troops on numerous disaster relief missions, at the same time, may stretch our capability and capacity."

The flow-on effect from worsening disasters can also create longer-term security challenges. After Black Summer, there were grave concerns for Sydney's water quality due to the damage across the Warragamba catchment as record rainfall washed ash and debris into streams and rivers. These challenges can persist, with the Cotter River catchment near Canberra still experiencing higher sediment loads well over a decade after major fires. Over Black Summer the electricity system in many places took a battering, from extreme heat degrading the operation of coal and gas power stations, bushfire smoke reducing the output from solar, to transmission infrastructure being damaged by fire and storms.

Our international reputation as a climate recalcitrant poses security and economic risks

Australia must prepare for this new era of megafires, intensifying droughts and floods, longer and hotter heatwaves, and the associated damage to our water supplies, infrastructure and critical industries, such as agriculture and tourism. This preparation, as well as recovery efforts, will be hugely expensive and require tough decisions about where to prioritise our resources. Of course it is not just Australia experiencing these threats. Over the last twenty years, Asia has experienced more ferocious and frequent extreme weather events than any other region, and most countries have fewer resources than Australia to prepare or recover. In 2020, some of the worst monsoon floods in decades hit much of Asia. In India, millions of people were displaced as 275,000 homes were destroyed or damaged and crops failed, while a quarter of Bangladesh was left under water. In the same way that Australia has had to add a new category of "catastrophic" to capture new conditions, Chandra Bhushan, who leads the International Forum for Environment, Sustainability and Technology in New Delhi, argues that India needs a new category to define the escalating intensity and volume of rainfall. Climate change is a "threat multiplier" adding pressure to existing problems that can contribute to destabilisation and conflict. The Australian Defence Force anticipates that as extreme weather worsens, the need for Australia to respond to disasters in our region will increase.

However, our vulnerability to the physical climate crisis is just one dimension. Increasingly, our lack of credible federal climate action and our international reputation as a climate recalcitrant also poses security and economic risks. For years now, European nations have discussed placing a cost on carbon-intensive imports, essentially ensuring that European Union industrial emitters are on a level playing field. Having received the backing of the European parliament, an EU Carbon Border Adjustment Mechanism is likely to begin in 2023. Joe Biden has also promised a US trade strategy that applies a "carbon adjustment fee" against countries that are "failing to meet their climate and environmental obligations to make sure that they are forced to internalize the environmental costs they're now imposing on the rest of the world". Similarly, UK prime minister Boris Johnson is reported to be considering using the G7 presidency to forge an alliance to apply penalties to countries with weak climate laws. Each of these proposals is designed to increase diplomatic and economic pressure on countries with insufficient emissions-reduction targets and high-intensity carbon economies. Australia fits the bill.

Pacific island nations are some of the most strident advocates for global climate action, given many face an existential threat from sea level rise, more powerful storms and other impacts of climate change. Australia's climate stance has caused considerable frustration among Pacific nations, but in the past their leverage has been primarily moral and diplomatic. With the growing Chinese engagement in the region, the Pacific is finding itself with potentially greater geopolitical power. While China's record on climate change is mixed, it has announced that it will peak its emissions before 2030 and has a 2060 target of carbon neutrality. There are concerns in security circles that Australia's lack of credible climate policy will harm our capacity for influence in the region, right at the time when it needs to be strong.

Perhaps the greatest error Australia is making internationally is dealing itself out of the conversation. In December 2020, Australia was snubbed at the Climate Ambition Summit, Boris Johnson's prelude to this year's United Nations Climate Change Conference in Glasgow, when it was denied the opportunity to address the summit. The reason: there continues to be no ambition or leadership from our federal government. Without a credible climate policy, we blunt our capacity to influence others, and will continue watching from the sidelines as other countries shape the 21st-century economic and geopolitical landscape.

During the decade or so of the "climate wars" in Australia, the conversation focused on whether climate change was happening, and if so, what it would cost to act. Meanwhile, the brutal reality of the vast and enduring consequences of inaction came to bear and we failed to grasp the enormous opportunities arising from the global transition to clean energy. As we have bickered, other countries have been moving on these opportunities, from renewable energy, battery storage, electric vehicles, clean hydrogen fuel, green manufacturing and more. As one of the sunniest and most resource-rich countries in the world, Australia has a natural competitive advantage. While some opportunities have been lost, with smart, consistent policy Australia can position itself to reap huge rewards from the clean energy revolution.

The opportunity in crisis

The Paris Agreement, which was made at the 2015 United Nations Climate Change Conference (COP21) in Paris, represented a major, long-term market signal. Countries, sub-national jurisdictions, business, industry and investors indicated they were aiming to get to net-zero emissions, virtually eliminating fossil fuel use. The sheer scale of investment across all sectors to meet this goal is mind-bogglingly large and represents an enormous restructuring of the global economy. These commitments also reflected the fact that the costs of renewable energy had fallen precipitously, and that in 2015 it already made both economic and environmental sense to shift investments from dirty to clean. Today this trend has only accelerated. Solar now offers "some of the lowest-cost electricity ever seen", the International Energy Agency reported in 2020, and is expected to match global coal output this decade.

Since the Paris Agreement was signed, global investment has moved from fossil fuels to climate solutions. In January 2020, BlackRock, the world's largest asset management firm, announced it was shifting its financial strategy to focus on climate change. They join 574 other investors in industry-led advocacy group Climate Action 100+, who collectively manage US$54 trillion

We should set our sights well beyond 100 per cent renewable energy use

in assets and are engaging companies on climate change governance and reducing emissions. This work dovetails into growing corporate action through many global and national initiatives. Under the international Science Based Targets initiative, more than 1000 companies, such as BMW, Kellogg's, HP and Nike, are pursuing emissions reductions in line with the climate science. Through RE100, a global initiative led by the Climate Group, 290 companies, including Unilever, Google and PepsiCo, have committed to reach 100 per cent renewable energy use. Many Australian companies, Qantas and Cbus among them, have followed this lead and committed to net-zero emissions or 100 per cent renewable energy use. This corporate leadership, which is occurring for economic, reputational and climate reasons, is resulting in a huge shift in capital. All this activity complements momentum through investment and good policy that is being driven by governments at national, state and local levels.

In a global environment where capital is looking for climate solutions, there are lots of opportunities for sunny Australia. Many expert commentators, such as Ross Garnaut and Australian Renewable Energy Agency boss Darren Miller, have reasoned that we should set our sights well beyond 100 per cent renewable energy use, towards 200, 500 or even 700 per cent. Indeed, Tasmania has already committed to achieve 200 per cent renewable energy. First, we can power our domestic electricity needs with cheap, reliable, clean electricity, using a mix of renewable energy and storage. Second, we can electrify most of our transportation and industrial processes, further expanding our renewable and storage deployment. And third – where it gets really exciting – we must start exporting our clean energy advantages to the world through an expansion of clean minerals processing, hydrogen fuel and even direct export of clean power into Asia. As Ross Garnaut notes in his 2019 book *Superpower*, Australia is the largest exporter of mineral ores such as steel, aluminium and iron, which require energy-intensive processing to be converted into metals. He argues that Australia, "in the post-carbon world", could become "the locus of energy-intensive processing of minerals for use in countries with inferior renewable energy resource endowments".

Australia also has major reserves in raw materials that will power the clean-energy revolution, including lithium, nickel, copper and rare earth metals. In a recent speech to the mining industry, the chair of Telsa, Robyn Denholm, noted that Tesla would soon annually consume more than $1 billion of Australian minerals to make their batteries and electric vehicles. She says, "Australia has the minerals to power the renewable energy age throughout the world in the coming years." Tesla estimates that in 2020 Australian lithium sold for about US$100 million ($129 million) – but if it was processed onshore in Australia, the value would have been more like US$1.7 billion. The rapid shift to renewable energy, batteries and electric vehicles as nations decarbonise will create a massive potential global market for Australian metals. While the federal government has provided a preliminary outline of a national minerals strategy, practical policies are urgently required to ensure Australia can make the most of our resources and know-how.

The momentum leading into Glasgow is our opportunity to pivot

There is growing momentum behind a vision for a clean power to define Australia's future prosperity, with a quiet revolution occurring at the local and state government levels. The climate tribalism that has been the unfortunate hallmark of federal politics is now largely absent at a state level, with significant leadership on climate change and clean energy being driven by Liberal governments in

South Australia and New South Wales. All Australian states have net-zero emissions-reduction targets, and all support renewable energy to varying degrees. This has been further accelerated through stimulus responses to COVID-19 – most state governments have introduced powerful policy packages to increase jobs, attract investment and tackle climate change simultaneously. In its recent Climate Change Action Plan, South Australia announced it could achieve more than 500 per cent of current grid demand in transforming its economy to net zero and becoming a major exporter of renewable energy. Similarly, 500 Australian cities and towns have committed to tackle climate change through the Cities Power Partnership.

The importance of state and local action should not be underestimated. Successful policies, targets and other initiatives at these levels are regularly copied by other jurisdictions, providing increasing scale. For instance, the Australian Capital Territory was the first jurisdiction to introduce a reverse-auction process to grow large-scale renewable energy projects. The policy was successful in helping the state reach its goal of 100 per cent renewable power by 2020, and has now been copied by states across Australia. The collective action by the states has been critical in reducing pollution in the electricity sector and increasing the uptake of renewable energy nationally. While Australia would benefit enormously from a coordinated national climate policy, the state governments are rightly not willing to miss out on the opportunities for jobs and investment by waiting indefinitely. Climate Council research with AlphaBeta in 2020 found that 76,000 jobs could be created across twelve areas over three years from good state government policies.

Successful action at a state and local level shows that the transition to a clean economy is possible and desirable. Projects are now underway around the country that demonstrate that renewable energy and storage projects provide jobs, regional opportunities and a stable, cheap power supply. Entrenched ideological positions against renewable power are now challenged by real-world results, and increasingly support for renewables is growing across the political spectrum. We have missed out on many opportunities by remaining wedded to the fossil fuel industry despite all evidence pointing to its inevitable and necessary demise. But state and local governments are providing blueprints for how Australia can capitalise on the opportunities presented by the clean energy revolution. Global momentum leading into the climate summit in Glasgow in November is a major opportunity for Australia to reposition itself from a global climate recalcitrant to a clean energy hub.

The Glasgow pivot

International agreements on climate change, as on other issues, rely on voluntary participation. They are built on trust and goodwill. Action by one nation can create a virtuous cycle leading to commitments from others, but selfishness can quickly undermine others' faith in the process. Like the twelve months prior to the Paris conference, 2021 sees a drumbeat of key international moments, both global and regional, leading up to Glasgow. These include the Biden–Harris Leaders Climate Summit, which was held in April; the release of the Intergovernmental Panel on Climate Change's Sixth Assessment Report from Working Group I, due in August; the Pacific Islands Forum, also in August; the UN General Assembly, in September; and the G20 Summit, in October. Each contributes momentum and goodwill for a successful outcome in Glasgow.

The Paris conference provided a formidable blueprint for creating international instruments that genuinely drive change. The Paris Agreement requires countries to continually increase their commitments, and in Glasgow they will be expected to strengthen 2030 emissions-reduction targets. Despite COVID-19 and a twelve-month delay in the conference, there has been a steady stream of national announcements. Glasgow's host nation, the United Kingdom, has committed to an emissions reduction of 68 per cent below 1990 levels by 2030, while the European Union has committed to at least a 55 per cent reduction. The growing list of countries committed to net zero by around mid-century now includes the three largest buyers of Australian coal and gas: China, Japan and South Korea. Combined, these three nations account for 41 per cent of our thermal coal exports and 50 per cent of our liquified natural gas exports. But perhaps the most important show has been from President Biden, which includes a US$2 trillion climate-focused infrastructure plan, and a promise to cut US carbon pollution in half by 2030. Biden has made it clear that climate change is at the top of his agenda and has appointed Paris veteran

John Kerry as Special Presidential Envoy for Climate. Kerry and his team wasted no time, using every diplomatic tool at their disposal to rally the world's major emitters to up their commitments ahead of Biden's Leaders Summit in April. The summit was fruitful, with many countries announcing increased 2030 commitments; for instance, Japan committed to reduce emissions by 46 to 50 per cent on 2013 levels, stronger than their existing 26 per cent reduction goal.

One of the most interesting dynamics of these global conferences is the constant dance between governments and all the other players – community groups, business, the media and so on. In the last few years, national action has generally been outstripped by action across

It is rumoured that Australia will announce net zero by 2050 [at] Glasgow

society, which in turn positively influences governments. During these events, such groups share information, build alliances and work together to push their national governments to do better. For instance, in 2014 the Global Covenant of Mayors was launched, providing an important platform for cities to encourage each other to strongly reduce emissions and pressure national governments.

It is rumoured that Australia will announce a net-zero by 2050 target as its contribution to the Glasgow conference. This would bring us into line with more than 100 countries and thousands of businesses and sub-national jurisdictions that have already committed to net zero.

While we should absolutely commit to net zero, we are being warned that the timeframe is out of step with the latest science. As the Climate Council's scientific report, "Aim High, Go Fast", states, "The world achieving net zero by 2050 is at least a decade too late and carries a strong risk of irreversible global climate disruption at levels inconsistent with maintaining well-functioning human societies."

The science is crystal clear that action taken this decade is critical, and that will be the focus of the Glasgow conference. Already the United States, Japan, the European Union and the United Kingdom have promised to halve emissions by 2030, making Australia's reduction target of 26 to 28 per cent look paltry. Despite these increased targets, and the acceleration of efforts across government, business and civil society, the sum of these efforts is still insufficient. They must continue to be scaled and accelerated so that we see the lion's share of emissions reductions happening this decade.

The latest scientific analysis from the Climate Council shows that Australia needs to reduce emissions by 75 per cent on 2005 levels by 2030. That may sound like a lot, and it is. But we must remember that there has been so little national action over the last thirty years that a slow response now represents accepting serious and devastating climate damage. To be credible in Glasgow, the Australian government needs to demonstrate that it can get emissions down dramatically this decade, including scaling up our 2030 target. We could match our allies by doubling our 2030 emissions-reduction target, or even better, we could align our targets with the imperative of protecting our citizens and go further.

Arriving in Glasgow with a net zero by 2050 target would be an embarrassing continuation of the Australian government's existing approach – that we will do the absolute bare minimum. This would be in keeping with having ratified the Kyoto Protocol a decade too late, even after we were given an extremely generous deal. Given our status as a major global emitter, it represents a dangerous normalisation of minimal effort to address a crisis that is now engulfing the world and should be at the top of our collective agenda.

There is such a thing as being too late

Martin Luther King's powerful address at Manhattan's Riverside Church in 1967 expressing his opposition to the Vietnam War is deeply applicable to the climate challenge we face today. "We are now faced with the fact that tomorrow is today," he said. "We are confronted with the fierce urgency of now. In this unfolding conundrum of life and history, there is such a thing as being too late. This is no time for apathy or complacency. This is a time for vigorous and positive action."

As I write this essay, I am in the final weeks before the birth of my second child. I'm conscious that he will never experience a time "before climate change", as the consequences are already all around us. We are certainly now too late to prevent some of the destruction that scientists warned of years ago, but the years ahead, particularly this decade, represent our best hope of passing on to my son's generation a stable world.

There has been a huge amount of commentary about the urgency of the climate crisis over the last two decades, and at times it can feel like just another issue, rather than a critical existential threat. Since the Bali conference, the world has moved significantly in the right direction. However, the scale and pace of change is not matching the scale and pace of the problem.

For Australia, there are serious risks to continuing our stance of largely ignoring the climate crisis. The federal government has a clear opportunity to follow the lead of state and local governments, scaling up their activities to capitalise on Australia's natural advantages in a clean-energy world. It is hard to imagine a country better placed to reap the economic rewards of one of the biggest industrial transformations the world has ever seen. With our sun, wind, open space and minerals, Australia could be a renewable superpower, creating significant opportunities for investment, job creation and regional growth.

With the Glasgow conference around the corner, Australia can reposition itself. This will give us more leverage to shape the global environment moving forward and to set ourselves up to meet the opportunities and challenges of the twenty-first century. Credible, serious commitments to get emissions down this decade must be central to that plan. Although I hope the federal government will make this pivot, even if they do not there are many opportunities for Australian businesses, local and state governments and civil society to extend their leadership and continue to push our nation in the right direction. The urgency of the climate crisis is such that it requires everyone to put their shoulder to the wheel, and we cannot wait. ■

THE FIX

Solving Australia's foreign affairs challenges

—

Anthony Bergin and Jeffrey Wall on How Australia Can Boost Business Ties with the Pacific

"Australia is losing ground in the fight for influence in the Pacific. We need a new approach, and fast."

THE PROBLEM: It's increasingly evident that our development assistance to the South Pacific isn't matching, let alone countering, China's increasingly aggressive intervention in the region.

This year, Australia is giving around AU$1.4 billion in aid to Pacific nations, including $600 million to Papua New Guinea (the largest recipient). Australia is also slowly distributing funding under the $2 billion Australian Infrastructure Financing Facility, the flagship initiative of Australia's Pacific Step-up.

China provides just under US$200 million a year in aid to Pacific nations, including around $100 million a year to Papua New Guinea. Why is China able to exert so much influence in the region given this comparatively low aid contribution?

The answer lies in the nature of its relationship with the island countries, especially those which have signed up to China's Belt and Road Initiative, such as Papua New Guinea, Vanuatu, Fiji, Cook Islands, Tonga and Samoa.

China does not achieve its agenda through development assistance. Its focus is on loans, principally for infrastructure, provided by the Exim Bank (the Export–Import Bank of China) and other Chinese finance institutions. Most of these loans have to be guaranteed by recipient governments.

The other condition on Belt and Road and related programs is that the work is undertaken by Chinese construction companies, chosen without any transparent tendering process. This can reduce the quality of the work and the benefits to the local economy through employment and provision of supplies and materials to the contractor. It also raises questions about whether Pacific island governments have been overlooking standard visa and work requirements.

In February 2021, for example, the Papua New Guinean government approved a guarantee of around K1 billion for a power line project from Yonki hydropower station in the nation's east to Mount Hagen, in the centre. The work went to a Chinese company with little or no experience in Papua New Guinea. Barely a week later, the government approved the separate K5-billion-plus Ramu 2 Hydro Electric Scheme. It was funded by an Exim Bank loan with a government guarantee via the state-owned

PNG Power, and awarded to a Chinese company. Australian and local companies weren't considered.

The problem for Australia, as it tries to compete with China's manoeuvring, is that over the last two decades there's been an exodus of Australian businesses – particularly larger companies – from the Pacific islands. Some of the departed businesses, such as construction companies Wagners and Barclays, Australian Family Assurance (previously Fiji Care), and Lleyton Holdings and Olex Cables (both now European-owned), had a substantial presence on the ground in multiple countries. Others were Australian companies that sold goods into the islands via Australian company representatives who knew all the owners and senior executives of local firms across the region.

More recently, Australian banks are selling out to smaller local operators. The departure of Westpac and the winding down of ANZ will have a dramatic effect on local economies. For more than 100 years, Australian banks and insurance companies have been the mainstay and leaders of Australian business in the region. Our banks have supported Pacific governments in their development activities and assisted them in arranging major international financial transactions and provided much-needed infrastructure finance. They've also been important sources of economic advice to the Australian government on the island countries.

Their withdrawal means a loss of personal contact between our private sector and island governments and communities.

It sends a message to other business that the Pacific isn't worth the candle and discourages Australian business from staying in or entering the region.

THE PROPOSAL: Australia needs a new partnership scheme between government and the Australian private sector, embracing South Pacific businesses as participants. The aim will be to encourage Australian businesses to operate in the Pacific without creating an uneven playing field for island companies. The partnership needs to offer more than affordable finance – it should offer grants that can directly challenge China's loans, which are ensnaring island nations in debt traps.

The Australian government needs to contribute at least AU$4 billion, with a mix of loans and grants, and offer funding to Australian construction and infrastructure companies to directly seek national and provincial government projects in Papua New Guinea and other Pacific countries such as Solomon Islands, Fiji and Vanuatu. The government should also insist that infrastructure projects be determined through a competitive and transparent tender process.

Affordable finance, with some government grants, will be more than competitive against Chinese loans, which require that work be undertaken by Chinese companies. The use of Chinese-tied funding has given China a stranglehold in the construction and telecommunications sectors, particularly in Papua New Guinea.

Australia should also take a tougher line with the Asian Development Bank and insist on a transparent process for all ADB projects. It's increasingly been awarding contracts to Chinese companies in the region, including for the upgrading of around twenty provincial airports across Papua New Guinea.

The Morrison government can't dictate which Australian businesses will operate in or service the Pacific. But it can influence outcomes by being more supportive and encouraging Pacific ventures by the private sector.

Australian government officials rarely consult or take Australian businesspeople with them to the region. When ANZ showed signs of leaving East Timor, then prime minister John Howard convinced them to stay. It would appear that this didn't happen when Westpac and ANZ announced plans to close operations in Fiji, Papua New Guinea, Tonga, Samoa, Cook Islands and Vanuatu.

The Australian government could support businesses interested in trading with Pacific countries. It could do this by improving double tax agreements or offering financial inducements, including import duty concessions.

To assist Australian business engagement in the region, Austrade's resources need strengthening in its Brisbane and Suva offices, and its office resources in Port Moresby should be maintained.

WHY IT WILL WORK: No matter how generous our aid to the region, it won't match, let alone counter, China's strategy of debt diplomacy and the growing influence of its Belt and Road agenda. The Australian Infrastructure Financing Facility, though commendable, isn't substantial enough, and its decision-making process is too cumbersome.

But Australia's response to the China challenge in the Pacific can't be based on loans alone. It must include grants that will be superior to China's loans in terms of affordability and attractiveness. Australia needs to assist its businesses to be the partner of choice for Pacific governments, businesses and consumers.

Measures to encourage Australian and Pacific business partnerships should consider the risk that these ventures may crowd out local businesses. Banks, locating processing centres and manufacturing plants that create jobs would be a good place to start. The Australian government should now be strengthening the existing Australian and island business councils and including them in its planning efforts.

There's no hope of excluding China from the region. But for our security, and that of our Pacific islands family, we need effective resistance aimed at reducing China's growing influence.

Australia is losing ground in the fight for influence in the Pacific. We need a new approach, and fast.

THE RESPONSE: The Minister for International Development and the Pacific, Zed Seselja, declined to comment.

Reviews

With the Falling of the Dusk: A Chronicle of the World in Crisis

Stan Grant

HarperCollins

GEOPOLITICS

Nostalgia has taken hold of Australian reporters who have covered China. For the first time since 1973, when Fairfax journalist Margaret Jones set up a Peking bureau in the thaw engineered by Chairman Mao and Comrade Gough, there is not a single Australian journalist in China working for an Australian outlet.

Consider that. China is hoovering up our iron ore at US$200-plus a tonne, while punishing our exporters of barley, timber, lobster and wine. Yet we have no direct public insight into our most powerful trading partner. Our ministers' calls go unanswered. The headlines beat on about "drums of war".

Our last two correspondents in China, forced to leave for their own safety in September 2020, both have books out: Bill Birtles' *The Truth About China* and Michael Smith's *The Last Correspondent*. Meanwhile, twenty-five former China correspondents have contributed essays to the collection *The Beijing Bureau*, edited by two of their number, Trevor Watson and Melissa Roberts.

Into this mix comes Stan Grant's *With the Falling of the Dusk*.

For twelve years, Grant lived in or reported on China. Best known for his work on Australian history, race and identity, Grant intriguingly nominates China as "the defining story of my career".

He brings to it, he asserts, a perspective not available to other Australians working this beat. "I am not of the West," he declares. "People of the West do not know what it is to face your own extinction." His Wiradjuri people know. So do the Chinese. Gazing from a passing train at a man working a horse-drawn plough, Grant reflects that he and the Chinese stranger both belong to "old cultures whose worlds have been upended by modernity".

A powerful passage examines the roots of nineteenth-century Chinese nationalism, as the Qing dynasty crumbled and European powers moved in, with a series of devastating incursions that led to domination of China's coastal trade. From this emerged Liang Qichao, the "godfather of Chinese nationalism". His intellectual disciple Sun Yat-sen – revered in modern China – saw the West's contempt for his people and feared for "the destruction of our race".

Today, Grant argues, an "existential sadness" underpins the Chinese Communist Party's determination to snub Western liberalism. Take Hong Kong's new national security laws, imposed after the territory's pro-democracy demonstrations. "Anyone who is the least bit surprised ... has not been paying attention," writes Grant. "How many times does the Communist Party leadership have to tell the West that it rejects liberal democracy before we will believe them?"

For Grant, the drive to efface humiliations imposed by the West is the motivating force for China. The Chinese will die before they are humiliated again, writes Grant.

China is "strong but paranoid, rich but not free ... a nation built on fear and top-down control". Bent on global domination, President Xi Jinping plans a military "capable of winning any war", domestically or internationally. But if most Chinese are better off materially than their parents, many also feel left behind in this land of instant millionaires, or long for more than economic dividends. Aware of this combustible element to the population, Xi portrays China as "a victim of the West" to bolster his power, because he needs external adversaries to sustain his control. "Xi knows he can always exploit a toxic nationalism."

The book is subtitled "A Chronicle of the World in Crisis", and the West does not escape censure. The United States, in Grant's view, is "broken" and "exhausted", incapable of countering China's rise. On firm display in these pages is Grant's ability to engage with the great philosophers – especially Georg Hegel, "the thinker who unlocks the door to so much of our world". Hegel believed history has an endpoint: when humans acquire full awareness of themselves and become free. Francis Fukuyama famously asked if the West had achieved it with the fall of the Berlin Wall. But if history does have a final state, Grant doubts it is liberal democracy. "Liberalism is in tatters," he argues, calling it "a timid faith, a tepid, bloodless idea". Indeed, he is doubtful on the state of humanity in general. "I am given to dark visions," he reflects at one point. "I have seen too much anger and violence, and I often fear that may be close to our true nature."

So there are no George Friedmanesque bromides here about America's triumphant ability to "work itself out in the murky depths". Instead, Grant launches a broadside on the failings of American neoliberalism and declares US president Joe Biden "part of the problem... a product of the same meritocracy that has sold out so many of its people". Members of this meritocracy have "rigged the game to suit themselves": "like the aristocrats, they party together, live alongside each other in the same wealthy suburbs, attend the same weddings", whereas "if you're born poor, you likely stay poor". The divide between the elites and the low-wage, low-hope masses has "deformed" American politics to the extent that the Land of Liberty "now stands as a symbol of democracy's decline".

Soon, for the first time in 300 years, the world's largest economy will not exist within a liberal democracy but under the control of a communist party-state confident in its authoritarianism. Between a rising, nationalistic China and a "fractured" America, Grant concludes, "our age is more dangerous and disordered than any period perhaps since the years before World War One". It is a sobering analysis, but not an unexpected one from someone who has spent years following this geopolitical tussle.

With the Falling of the Dusk is a true reporter's book, rich in the detail that more academic analyses lack. Take Grant's encounter with a Pakistani Taliban suicide-bomber recruiter, left chained in the sun while awaiting execution:

> He spoke so slowly and softly that I had to lean forward to hear him. Close, close enough that I could feel his breath. I could see now how he used that power to draw people in, to bring them under his spell so that he could enter their hearts and their minds. Closer... lean in closer ... then he's got you.

On the Yellow River, Grant meets Lun Lun, a fisherman whose catch these days is human bodies – the remains of the suicides flowing downstream from the provincial capital, Lanzhou. "The speed of life had overtaken many," Grant observes. "Families were falling apart under the strain, and there was increasing isolation, anxiety and depression. China did not have time to reach back for those who could not keep up."

In a book that traverses not only China and the West, but also militant Islam and even North Korea, one looming issue gets little attention: Taiwan. I know Grant, so I rang him. When I ask him to clarify his view on Taiwan's likely fate, he tells me he agrees with strategist Hugh White that a war over Taiwan could go nuclear: "No one wins. It would be unimaginable – a failure on all sides." Aside from the unlikely collapse of the Communist Party, China's trajectory is set: "to return to the world as a great power, with the exceptionalism that great powers demand – and with that comes the inevitability of reunification with Taiwan. The best we can do is buy time."

Grant writes lyrically about the world, but his vision is a bleak one. The evidence from NATO and the G7 is that the Western powers are hedging on the basis that he might be right.

Hugh Riminton

The War on the Uyghurs: China's Internal Campaign against a Muslim Minority
Sean R. Roberts
Princeton University Press

One morning in 2003, I ran into a boy flogging newspapers energetically outside the gate of Xinjiang University. "Good news!

Häsän Mäkhsum is dead!" The name didn't ring any bells for me, but the article identified him as the mastermind of an "East Turkistan Islamic Movement", an organisation the American government had recently listed as a terrorist organisation. America's decision to do so lent significant credibility to China's claims to be prosecuting a "war on terror" in Xinjiang.

Two decades on, this war has come to pervade and restructure the whole of Xinjiang society. Academics I was studying with in 2003 have disappeared; re-education camps have taken in friends and their relatives. China's war on terror, Roberts argues in this timely book, is better thought of as a "war on the Uyghurs".

When was this war first declared? From its first incorporation into the Qing empire in the 1750s, Roberts sees Beijing's relationship to this predominantly Muslim, Turkic-speaking region as a colonial one. It was in the 1990s, though, that the region shifted from the status of a "frontier colony" – a zone of relative neglect – to a "settler colony", with all the drive to assimilate and integrate that this term entails. Although noting various points in China's modern history

where some stable accommodation to local difference might have been negotiated, he is pessimistic about that possibility today.

While a strong critic of the "terror-watching" mode of analysis, Roberts knows the obscure world of Uyghur militancy better than most: he has interviewed Uyghurs who languished in Guantanamo Bay and has met members of Uyghur militias in Syria. The book combs through Chinese and Western media, as well as obscure jihadist websites, to provide the most comprehensive narrative available of the last two decades of sporadic violent incidents in Xinjiang and the Chinese state's response to them.

Its conclusions are sceptical: militant Uyghur networks have been ephemeral and ineffective, and their role has been exaggerated for political purposes – internationally, to win acceptance of China's role in a global "war on terror", and domestically, to justify ever more invasive policies of surveillance and indoctrination.

In fact, Roberts argues, very little of the violence in Xinjiang should be considered "terrorism" at all. To make this point, he employs a definition that limits the term to deliberate attacks on civilians. It's a defensible, but possibly controversial, view. If a government-appointed imam is assassinated in Kashgar, for example, is there much to be gained by insisting that this is *not* a form of terrorism?

The obvious worry is that too much talk of terrorism gives credence to China's claims to be engaged in a legitimate counterterrorism campaign. But the semantic debate may distract from the wider critique of the counterterrorism paradigm that the book is making: that incidents of violence reflect political grievances – old and new – which the "terrorist" moniker obscures, and that Beijing's actions reflect long-standing anxieties about ethnic and religious difference that it now wishes to resolve once and for all. The global "counterterrorism industrial complex" that Roberts describes as shaping international opinion has been replicated in China. Chinese officials at various levels may imagine themselves pursuing measures to stem violent attacks, but counterterrorism is best thought of as a modality of contemporary Chinese settler colonialism, not a motivation for it.

Public knowledge of the crisis in Xinjiang has grown in Australia, but it is yet to produce much in the way of a policy response. Recommendations to legislate Magnitsky sanctions – sanctions on individuals implicated in significant human rights abuses – seem to have been shelved. South Australian senator Rex Patrick's push to combat non-voluntary labour programs with a ban on imports from Xinjiang has elicited vague promises of a future review of the *Modern Slavery Act 2018*, which requires large corporations operating in Australia to report annually on conditions for workers within their supply and delivery chains.

While some governments have heeded calls to recognise China's policies as "genocide", Australia and New Zealand have declined to do so. Roberts himself avoids the term, limiting his critique to "cultural genocide". The debate has left advocacy groups in something of an awkward position. While Human Rights Watch found insufficient evidence for the genocide charge (describing China's abuses as "crimes against humanity"), its China director has nevertheless encouraged governments to endorse it.

This emphasis on terminology reflects hope that international law might offer some remedy to the plight of the Uyghurs. That is questionable, though, not only because of China's strength, but also because of Western actions that have undermined the functioning of institutions such as the International Criminal Court. America's May 2021 veto of UN condemnation of Israel's shelling of the Gaza Strip gave China an opportunity to posture as the defender of international norms.

These are depressing realities for anyone looking to international action to alleviate the suffering in Xinjiang, and Roberts is conscious of them. His hope is for a popular movement capable of pressuring China, something akin to the anti-apartheid campaign against South Africa.

It's a sentiment I share, but it can be a difficult proposition to put to Uyghurs. US–China tensions have given their advocates entrée to the corridors of Washington decision-making. To shift towards a grassroots solidarity campaign might well seem undesirable, not to mention far-fetched.

This is where debates surrounding Xinjiang in progressive circles take on importance. A vibrant, standalone campaign for Uyghur rights is indeed a remote possibility, but small movements can ally with big movements. While Cold War politics conditions us to particularise, and keep the focus exclusively on China, the progressive instinct is to generalise and draw links on the basis of common principles. Today, when opposition to racism and Islamophobia finds expression on a global scale – as, for example, in the Black Lives Matter movement, or the upsurge of support for the Palestinians – it becomes possible to imagine what it might look like to generalise these principles and extend their focus to China.

To be sure, this perspective meets resistance from certain "anti-imperialists" who defend or downplay the oppression in Xinjiang, but Roberts' book serves as a response to this special pleading. As he demonstrates amply, China's war on terror is no humane alternative to the West's, but an extreme application of the same violent, dehumanising logic.

David Brophy

Until the World Shatters: Truth, Lies, and the Looting of Myanmar
Daniel Combs
Melville House

I t is impossible to read Daniel Combs' excellent *Until the World Shatters* without reflecting on the current crisis unfolding in Myanmar. The book was released in March this year, just a few weeks after the military, led by General Min Aung Hlaing, detained the country's de facto leader, Aung San Suu Kyi, along with elected National League of Democracy (NLD) political leaders, on charges of electoral fraud. In response, huge numbers of ordinary Myanmar people joined the countrywide civil disobedience movement, refusing to work in order to disrupt the economy and halt the flow of funds to the junta. Their peaceful protests have been met with a disproportionate level of violence. To date, over 700 protestors have been killed and more than 5000 detained. Yet the movement continues, albeit on a smaller scale.

As I watch the news and read the social feeds from friends and colleagues in Myanmar (when their internet is working), what strikes me over and over again is the role of the young in leading this struggle. Women and men, mostly in their twenties, organise protests over social media and put themselves on the frontline to face police bullets. In recent weeks, they have been "going into the forest", a euphemism for joining the People's Defence Force. They have seen what their parents and grandparents endured during the worst years of the junta. They lived through Myanmar's transformative liberalisation. They know only too well that if the coup succeeds, they will lose everything.

Until the World Shatters follows the perspectives of two young men around the same age as many of Myanmar's civil defence movement protesters. Combs, who was in his twenties when he researched this book, uses their stories to immerse the reader in the complex realities of pre-coup Myanmar.

Phoe Wa is a talented photographer who has talked his way into an unpaid and unofficial internship as a photojournalist at *Myanmar Times*, an English- and Myanmar-language newspaper headquartered in Yangon, the nation's largest city. A country boy from the Mon province in the southeast, he is politely self-effacing and short of both funds and friends. Not much help for getting ahead in pushy, worldly Yangon.

By contrast, Bum Tsit seems well on his way to becoming a big shot in Kachin State, in Myanmar's mountainous north. His family owns a popular restaurant as well as a jewellery shop, and he drives a luxury Toyota Kluger. He also volunteers at the Red Cross, helping out at the camps for internally displaced people. Thanks to his native intelligence and almost bottomless charm, he mixes as easily with Kachin independence fighters as with NLD government officials and former military colonels. This is surprising; since 1948, Kachin militias have been fighting government forces for sovereignty over these mountains in the world's longest-running civil war. Bum Tsit longs to do something tangible for his war-ravaged people.

Maybe he will enter politics one day. If he is to realise this ambition, he will need serious money. And so he enters the murky jade trade.

Combs' choice of protagonists allows him to focus on two of Myanmar's key issues. The first, the failure of Myanmar's media to report the truth due to deep-seated ethnic, religious and racial bias. The second, the ongoing theft of natural resources by the country's elite at the expense of services and infrastructure.

The book is set in 2017 and coincides with the ethnic cleansing of the Rohingya. That year, around 700,000 Rohingya fled their homes in the southwest province of Rakhine for refugee camps in Bangladesh. Decades of propaganda characterised the Rohingya as "illegal Bengali immigrants" rather than a people of Myanmar with rights to citizenship (Myanmar operates a tiered citizenship system linked to racial identity). The term "Rohingya" became taboo, and even privately owned English-language newspapers such as *Myanmar Times* refused to use it. Reuters journalists Wa Lone (who once worked for *Myanmar Times*) and Kyaw Soe Oo were arrested for reporting on military massacres in the Rakhine village of Inn Din. They were held for 500 days. All journalists feared they too would be jailed if they reported on the atrocities being inflicted on the Rohingya people.

Anti-Muslim feeling runs deep in the country. Combs attempts to delve into the reasons for this, and spends time in the Yangon music and arts scene. Witnessing a concert showcasing local punk, heavy metal and rap, Combs captures an eclectic, free-thinking and anti-authority crowd of trans women, hip-hop dancers and heavy metal fans with dyed mohawks. He notes that the concerts can be organised in a matter of hours, a feat made possible by the exponential take-up of the internet in the country. At one point, the punk band Side Effect divides the audience into two and demands they shout "I hate you" and "I love you" at each other. Then they launch into a song "about Meikhtila", site of a sectarian massacre, where Buddhists targeted Muslims in 2013. "This is the truth that our government doesn't want us to know," a young man tells Combs. Government censorship may have been dismantled in 2012, but the habits of not speaking up in case of arrest, of keeping quiet,

of self-censorship, are hard to break. Still, it seems ironic that the explosion of the internet (in particular Facebook, which *is* the internet in Myanmar) has enabled these radicals and free-thinkers to find one another in Yangon. Facebook was also a key source of rampant unchecked anti-Muslim propaganda in the campaign of hatred against the Rohingya. Social media has only amplified the extreme emotions fizzing through Myanmar's transforming society.

Combs' detailed reporting on the little-covered underground economy of the jade trade in Kachin State anchors the narrative. Profits from resources such as natural gas have lined the pockets of generals and their cronies (businesspeople with ties to the military) for generations. However, the unique properties of jade make it not only incredibly valuable but also a perfect vehicle for black-market trade. Imperial jade, of which Myanmar has the world's largest reserve, is a vibrant green and highly prized by China's uber rich. Combs gives the example of a Myanmar jadeite necklace that sold for US$27 million in 2012. The value of jade is fluid, based entirely on aesthetic perception rather than karats or weight. For this reason, this precious stone offers an almost perfect means for evading taxes and laundering money. As one seasoned trader explains it, he could sell a jade ornament for $2000 but write a receipt for $20 because there is "no way for regulators to check".

Combs puts the value of the jade trade between China and Myanmar in the tens of billions, or between 23 and 62 per cent of the country's gross domestic product. Jade has financed the Kachin Independence Army since the 1960s; it also lines the pockets of Myanmar's military officers. These two sides may be antagonists in the world's longest-running civil war, but they'll cooperate in the interest of digging up as much of the stone as possible to sell to the highest bidder before regulation comes.

Combs traces the debilitating effects of this rampant theft on the country. The loss of land to jade mining turns landowners into subsistence miners. Fighting for control of and access to the trade has displaced more than 100,000 people. In the absence of local medical care, Combs's Kachin *bazaar mamma*, an elderly woman who sells him fruit each time he visits, must make an expensive trip to Yangon, where the only way to see a doctor is to bribe the poorly paid nursing staff. (How poorly paid are medical staff? My aunty, a retired obstetrician, told me that the fee she used to receive for delivering a healthy child in the public system was equivalent to her patient's bus fare home from the hospital.)

It is the personal losses and gains that are most moving. Bum Tsit and Phoe Wa may be from Myanmar's marginal states and face extraordinary challenges, but they are also ordinary guys. They like drinking beer, talking about their girlfriends, listening to music and spinning plans for the future. Ultimately, the most poignant comparison is between the author and his subjects – one cannot help but wonder what Phoe Wa and Bum Tsit, with all their natural abilities, might do with the opportunities Combs has had. Myanmar favours the elite, which means these men have to fight hard for their achievements. The system in which they live feels stacked against them. As Phoe Wa comments: "For every one step that they walk, I have to walk five."

I finished this moving, impeccably researched book wondering what had become of Phoe Wa and Bum Tsit, the *bazaar mamma*, the Yangon punk rocker and all the other vivid, ordinary, engaging people in its pages. How have they fared in an increasingly violent Myanmar?

One line stayed with me.

"It doesn't matter if you are Kachin or Bamar or Shan or Lisu, if you are weak, you suffer. If you are powerful, you take."

Let's hope the young protesters of Myanmar are able to change this.

Michelle Aung Thin

Correspondence

"Enter the Dragon"
by John Keane

Fergus Ryan

n his dense yet sprawling essay "Enter the Dragon" (AFA11: *The March of Autocracy*), political scientist John Keane explores the features of what he dubs China's "phantom democracy" and looks ahead to its implications for the country's expanding "galaxy empire".

Keane's contention, first stated in his 2017 book *When Trees Fall, Monkeys Scatter*, is that the Chinese Communist Party (CCP) maintains its power in China not so much through the barrel of a gun as through its use of opinion polls, village elections and social media as a listening post to gauge what the citizenry wants. "In the PRC, state violence and repression are masked," Keane writes. "Coercion is calibrated: cleverly camouflaged by elections, public forums, anticorruption agencies and other tools of government with a 'democratic' feel."

What Keane misses is that many of the features of his imagined "phantom democracy" in China are either relics of the "semi-liberal" era under General Secretary Hu Jintao, which dated from 2002 to 2012, or have long been mirages that are dissipating as the country grows strong enough to invest more heavily in the tools and infrastructure required for maintaining ideological control.

According to Keane, China's "phantom democracy" can be seen in the behaviour of Xi Jinping, who presses the flesh like politicians in liberal democracies, as well as in village elections and the spread of "consultative democracy" into "city administration and business". This approach, he suggests, may soon extend to how China deals with the rest of the world. China's leaders may be able to succeed "not only in harnessing phantom democratic mechanisms at home to legitimate and strengthen their single-party rule, but also abroad, in the far-flung districts of their empire".

Before we get too carried away with imagined futures, it's instructive to note how Beijing is currently attempting to keep other countries in the orbit of its "galaxy empire". The Chinese embassy in Canberra's leak of "fourteen disputes" to the Australian media in November 2020 is a good place to start. More a list of demands than disputes, it included calls for Canberra to muzzle our free press, suppress news critical of China, sell off strategic assets and roll back laws designed to counter Beijing's covert influence operations here.

The release of the demands and Beijing's subsequent deployment of coercive economic leverage on Australia has flung us further away from China's gravitational pull. Since its release, the Morrison government has doubled down on a strategy of selective decoupling from China by cancelling the Victorian government's Belt and Road Initiative agreement with Beijing. The Northern Territory's ninety-nine-year lease of Darwin Port to Chinese company Landbridge may very well be next.

The title of Keane's 2017 book is taken from a Chinese proverb he says is top of mind for the CCP leadership from Xi Jinping down, because they fear that if the party falls, the economic, social and political repercussions for the country would be catastrophic. Another simian-related Chinese idiom is no doubt on the tip of their tongues as they consider how to fend off this calamity: killing the chicken to scare the monkeys.

It's doubtful that Beijing ever expected Canberra to reverse course on any of the grievances leaked by the embassy. In the eyes of China's leaders, Australia is the chicken, and they fully intend to make an example of us as a warning to other countries considering challenging the People's Republic of China. The reality is that the CCP is no more interested in winning over the consent of other countries than in gaining the approval of its own citizens. You either fall in line or become tomorrow's roast chook.

No sooner had Keane published his book in 2017 than the wheels of his argument began to fall off. Time limits on officeholders was included as a feature of his "phantom democracy", but does not make an appearance in this recent iteration of his argument after Xi Jinping effectively appointed himself emperor for life. But the linchpin of Keane's "phantom democracy" argument is the country's use of village elections as a form of "consultative democracy". The problem with this argument is that village elections have been systematically undermined by Beijing for twenty years and have now been effectively abolished.

First introduced in the 1980s, village elections proved an effective way of improving local governance, but were steadily sidelined in importance as China's economy grew and the central government was able to dramatically increase investment in its bureaucratic capacity, according to long-time election watchers Monica Martinez-Bravo of CEMFI (Center for Monetary and Financial Studies), Gerard Padró i Miquel of Yale University, Nancy Qian of Northwestern University and Yang Yao of Peking University. "Why would the Chinese government in the 2000s systematically undermine local elections, which we document to have been effective in improving local governance?" the quartet write in their 2017 paper "The Rise and Fall of Local Elections in China". "Our study suggests a simple explanation: if the autocrat can afford better direct control, then it does not need to suffer the policy costs associated with electoral monitoring."

The same principle is at play in Beijing's attempts to bring its bustling social media sphere to heel. Under Hu, online platforms such as Weibo acted as a pressure valve whenever public opinion boiled over. Under Xi, more direct control is possible: surveillance has increased, and the censorship burden has shifted from the internet companies to the users themselves. The project is in a nascent form, but the contours are clear – the internet is to be harnessed as a tool of omniscient control, not as some passive listening post feeding back to the Mandarins in Zhongnanhai.

It's evident to anyone engaged with Chinese social media that the already narrow space to speak freely online has shrunk considerably under Xi Jinping. In February 2021, China's internet regulator started to require bloggers to have a government-approved credential before they could publish on a wide range of subjects that extend beyond politics and military topics to health, economics, education and judicial matters. That's just one of the latest examples of the CCP's attempts to increase its stranglehold over the Chinese internet. But the strategy goes beyond mere censure. It's now no longer enough to steer clear of certain topics; it's everyone's responsibility to emphasise uplifting messages over criticism – referred to by the CCP as spreading "positive energy" – and engage in national boosterism or "telling China's story well", as Xi instructed in his report to the 19th CCP National Congress in 2017.

Until the early years of the Xi era there had always been enough of a democratic patina in the party's rhetoric and the PRC's structure to fool the odd CEO, prime minister or visiting scholar. Not only does the PRC have a parliament; it also has a judiciary and eight legally recognised parties. This belief has long since dissipated from boardrooms and party rooms and yet appears to persist in academia. One wonders how long it will be before some scholars stop pretending China is a democracy, phantom or not.

Fergus Ryan is an analyst with the Australian Strategic Policy Institute's International Cyber Policy Centre.

Kevin Boreham

I n his tough-minded essay on China's return to world pre-eminence, John Keane assesses how China "throws its cultural weight around on the global stage" while domestically "[t]he slightest whiff of a challenge to the CCP's power can bring down the hammer". China's aggressive rejection of human rights is the result of three decades of indifference to its human rights violations from the international community, including Australia, as nations pursued the riches flowing from China's economic opening.

In March 2021, geopolitical strategist Robert D. Kaplan wrote in *Foreign Policy*, "China knows that in a world where everyone trades with it – and therefore requires, at some level, its approval – states will pay lip service to human rights while acting on their economic interests."

Western and other like-minded states, including Australia, have long acquiesced in excluding China's human rights violations from UN action. Back in 1997, China blocked a resolution over its human rights abuses in the UN Commission on Human Rights, the forerunner of the UN Human Rights Council. The United States and the European Union sent signals even before the commission meeting that they would not stand up to China over this: the EU procrastinated on how it would deal with the issue, while Washington indicated that Sino–US relations would not be "held hostage" to human rights concerns. Since then, there has been no effective consideration of holding China to account in an international forum.

China regards Geneva, where the UN Human Rights Council meets, as its front line. No one who has observed China's tough, effective and well-resourced efforts to suppress any consideration of its human rights record could doubt that China takes the deliberations of UN human rights bodies very seriously.

Keane aptly shows that the Chinese leadership embraces a "phantom democracy" governing style that is entirely superficial and entirely geared to maintain the control of the CCP. His discussion of the mechanisms of control – data-harvesting through the *People's Daily* Online Public Opinion Monitoring Centre and opinion polling through organisations such the Canton Public Opinion Research Centre (C-por) – is illuminating.

China's strategy in multilateral bodies, particularly the Human Rights Council, complements the manipulation of domestic opinion that Keane identifies. China builds common interests with other states that also have poor records of democratic governance and observance of human rights. A 2017 Human Rights Watch report observed China's tendency to marshal support from developing countries "by strategically positioning itself as [their] champion" and "defending them in the Council when they receive specific attention".

There has been token pushback against China's aggressive stance over criticism of its human rights record. In March 2016, Australia issued a joint statement with eleven other states at the Human Rights Council criticising China's "deteriorating human rights record". In July 2019, twenty-two countries, including Australia, formally urged China to end its mass arbitrary detentions and related violations against Muslims in the Xinjiang region.

Most significantly, during the latest council meeting, in March 2021, seventy countries signed a statement by Belarus that supported China's policy towards Hong Kong, noting that "non-interference in internal affairs of sovereign states is an important principle enshrined in the Charter of the United Nations and a basic norm governing international relations". A joint statement led by the United States and signed by fifty-three nations including Australia rebutted this position, asserting that "states that commit human rights violations must be held to account". This statement reflects the human rights policy of the Biden–Harris administration. Secretary of State Antony Blinken, speaking at the launch of the department's annual "Country Reports on Human Rights Practices" on 30 March, confirmed that "we will bring to bear all the tools of our diplomacy to defend human rights and hold accountable perpetrators of abuse".

We will have to see how this determination to hold to account human rights violators plays out in relation to other national interests. For the moment, as the International Service for Human Rights commented about previous joint statements, they "fall short of decisive action".

Meanwhile, China has skilfully proposed alternatives to the Geneva process. A diplomat whose country engages in bilateral human rights dialogues with China told Human Rights Watch in 2017 that some observers thought the Chinese government used approval for the next human rights dialogue "like a cookie", agreeing to a date only when the other parties had refrained from publicly issuing human rights criticism.

In 1997, Australia agreed to start a formal and regular bilateral dialogue on human rights with China. The dialogue has become mute: the last round of the Australia–China Human Rights Dialogue was held in February 2014. This preference for more easily controllable bilateral channels on human rights was implied in the 2017 Foreign Policy White Paper, which states that "Australia will promote human rights through constructive bilateral dialogue".

These weak reactions to China's human rights violations have reinforced what Keane calls "China's greatest flaw: its lukewarm and contradictory embrace of public accountability mechanisms". They show the need for the process fellow essayists in the issue, Natasha Kassam and Darren Lim, urge: "working with partner states to develop clear parameters of unacceptable behaviour [by China], particularly on … egregious human rights violations". More generally, they show the dire consequences of soft options in responding to gross human rights violations.

Kevin Boreham has been DFAT assistant secretary, South-East Asia branch, and assistant secretary, International Organisations branch, and taught international law at the Australian National University.

John Keane responds

I thank Kevin Boreham and Fergus Ryan for their comments on my essay. Both authors are silent about its principal aim – to offer a fresh interpretation of China's emerging role as a global empire. They are instead exercised by single issues. Their analysis of these is disappointing, and the consequences less than satisfying.

Kevin Boreham, a former public servant and scholar of international law, is preoccupied with human rights. His comments are important, for they remind us of the continuing political importance of the marriage of the languages of human rights and democracy that happened for the first time during the late 1940s. The crowning achievement of that decade was the Universal Declaration of Human Rights. Drafted in 1947–48 in response to genocide in the aftermath of global war, its preamble spoke of "the inherent dignity" and "the equal and inalienable rights of all members of the human family". The declaration – the most translated document ever, available nowadays in 500 languages – proclaimed a series of inalienable rights for everyone, "without distinction of any kind, such as race, colour, sex, language, religion, political or other opinion, national or social origin, property, birth or other status".

Boreham is aware that the project of guaranteeing that every human being enjoys the right to have rights remains utopian. It is unfinished business – he could have added – often because of the human rights games played by states. Human rights attract swindlers, prevaricators and peddlers of double standards. Boreham wags his finger at China's "aggressive rejection of human rights". He underscores China's "tough, effective and well-resourced efforts to suppress any consideration of its human rights record". He has a point, but things are more complicated than his let's-pick-a-fight-with-China reasoning supposes. It should be remembered that China has consistently emphasised the *social* dimensions of human rights. In this it finds justification in the wording of the original declaration, which envisaged a world in which human beings enjoy "freedom from fear and want". It's why vaccines, healthcare, education, transportation and anti-poverty programs are among China's policy priorities at home and abroad. Human rights in this selective sense are its thing – and a key reason why the PRC regime generates loyalty at home and respect abroad, in such regions as Central Asia and sub-Saharan Africa. Worth bearing in mind too is that there are moments when China takes the lead on gross human rights abuses, as happened recently when China, president of the Security Council for the month of May 2021, was joined by Norway and Tunisia in issuing a public statement and call for action to remedy the injustices produced by Israel's continuing colonisation of territory and cruel military attacks on Palestinians.

Where was Australia and its buddy the United States during this grave moment? They fell silent, and not for the first time. Australian governments have a habit of dining on double standards. As Boreham observes, they do issue magniloquent statements at the Human Rights Council denouncing China's "egregious human rights violations". What he doesn't tell us is that Australia has so far not signed the International Labour Organization treaty on forced labour. Or that detention camps have long been a feature of refugee policy. Or that at home Australia's democracy and human rights standards are disfigured by the erosion of civil liberties, the failure to build a federal anti-corruption commission, denials of political representation of Indigenous peoples and failures to grant voting rights for our permanent residents. The long and lengthening list of double standards surely contains an important general lesson: governments that want to preach human rights effectively should also make every effort to practise human rights with a strong measure of self-consistency.

Fergus Ryan's remarks are disappointing, coming as they do from a policy researcher at the Australian Strategic Policy Institute, the government-funded think tank that claims to be an independent, non-partisan body producing timely, expert advice for Australia's foreign policy and military leaders. Ryan ignores virtually all the carefully detailed propositions tabled in my essay. The notion of a galaxy empire; the Belt and Road Initiative; China's emergent global communications networks; its unconventional military strategy and commitment to cross-border institution building: these and other themes are single-mindedly set aside.

Ryan has only one aim: to hammer on about my phantom democracy argument, first outlined (as he notes) in *When Trees Fall, Monkeys Scatter* (2017) and developed more recently (which he does not acknowledge) in *The New Despotism* (2020). He manages to misrepresent both the core meaning of the phrase "phantom democracy" and the subtle details of how the CCP regime tries to overcome information shortages and learn from information disputes ("digital mutinies", I call them) at home and abroad. Ryan wants readers to believe that the current regime is based on brute force and fear, that the CCP leadership cares nothing for the arts of winning the loyalty of its subjects. This leads him to ignore the well-documented evidence of the skittishness of the CCP rulers, their anxiety about the dangers of losing popular support. China is instead mistakenly portrayed as a polity in which the rulers ride roughshod over their cowed subjects. The CCP's sophisticated use of public opinion polls, online public forums, local mobile courts and other techniques of governing is deemed irrelevant. This tempts Ryan into supposing, again mistakenly, with hints of Orientalist prejudice, that China's people are merely sheepish objects of "omniscient control". They tell no jokes, never complain about abuses of power, swallow propaganda and mindlessly celebrate ethically significant rituals such as the annual Dragon Boat Festival (a public holiday commemorating the scholar Qu Yuan, who suicided after being wronged by a third-century BCE emperor).

Ryan isn't interested in complications. China-baiting is his mother tongue. His single-minded mission is to portray China as a serious threat to global order and peace, to join those who now bang the local drums of war. Hence the crudity of his comments. Repeating the well-known Chinese proverb about killing chickens to scare monkeys, he comments: "In the eyes of China's leaders, Australia is the chicken, and they fully intend to make an example of us as a warning to other countries considering challenging the People's Republic of China. The reality is that the CCP is no more interested in winning over the consent of other countries than in gaining the approval of its own citizens. You either fall in line or become tomorrow's roast chook."

This is bogan political thinking. It spreads bigotry and gets people used to the smell of blood and destruction. Prejudice of its kind is socially divisive, politically irresponsible and militarily dangerous, my essay tried to show. Its niceties evidently failed to persuade Fergus Ryan, which prompts me to reach for John A. Hobson's *The Psychology of Jingoism* (1901), an old but incisive account with a new relevance on the perils of jingoist stereotyping of foreign powers. And to dedicate to Mr Ryan my impromptu ode to asinine unreason:

> *We don't want to fight but by Jingo if we do*
> *We've got the subs, the planes and men, as well as money too*
> *We've kicked them out before, so while we're Aussies true*
> *Them Chinese won't ever get their yellow hands on me and you.*

John Keane is politics professor at the University of Sydney and the author of The Life and Death of Democracy.

"Future Shock" by Natasha Kassam and Darren Lim

Yun Jiang

Natasha Kassam and Darren Lim's essay "Future Shock" (AFA11: *The March of Autocracy*) presents an accurate portrayal of China's political system. It sees China with clear eyes, but fails to see ourselves and our ally with the same clear eyes.

Let's take the term "liberal international order", which is ubiquitous in the article. The authors write about the postwar liberal international order in glowing terms. But the order was only liberal from the perspective of the dominant powers – the West that we're part of.

Like many in Australia, Kassam and Lim look to the past with rose-tinted glasses. We tend to forget that under the so-called "liberal" order, the United States and its partners supported the overthrow of democratically elected governments in countries such as Iran and Guatemala. Its interventions in the Middle East (far from the US homeland) continue to this day. "Liberal rules and norms" were quickly brushed aside when they became inconvenient.

So I disagree with Kassam and Lim that "international orders reflect the character of the great powers that found and lead them". Liberal democracies are just as proficient as illiberal states at using illiberal and coercive means to force their will on others.

Being a democracy at home did not stop the United States from supporting the authoritarian regime in Saudi Arabia. Nor did the United States push for more human rights for Palestinians even though it has significant influence on Israel as its biggest supporter.

The authors are adept at excusing the illiberal behaviour of the United States, explaining, in one instance, that it is "for the narrow purpose of protecting an ally" rather than "weakening the rights themselves". But for countries on the receiving end, what difference does that make? Can China not claim a similar privilege? How can we speak of "rights" or "rules and norms" when they can be ignored or violated by the great powers at will?

If the United States is perfectly willing to work with authoritarian regimes and dictatorships and overlook human rights concerns, then China can also cooperate with democracies. International orders may not always reflect the character of the great powers that found and lead them. China becoming more powerful does not necessarily mean that it will seek to impose its governance system on other countries through coercion.

In fact, China is behaving like rising powers before it, including the United States. China's interests are expanding. It seeks increasing power and influence in its neighbourhood, which it sees as its sphere of interest.

Kassam and Lim attribute growing concerns about China in Australia to China's authoritarian governance system and the threat it poses to the "liberal international order". But would a democratic China be less ambitious or less driven to assert its ever-expanding suite of global interests?

Indeed, Australia and the United States were also very concerned about rising Japan in the 1980s. Back then, Japan was seen as a threat to the American economy and condemned for "unfair trade". In Australia, growing Japanese investment faced a strong backlash. Sound familiar? Yet Japan was a US ally and a democracy.

Perhaps part of the reason we are so anxious is that China (like Japan) is not an Anglosphere power. Instead, it is an Asian power.

We are worried because we (the West) may no longer be at the top of the pecking order. We are experiencing what it feels like to be coerced, to be interfered with. We are experiencing a small taste of what it is like to be a country in South America or the Middle East or South-East Asia. And, unsurprisingly, we don't like it.

It is not about China versus the West, it's about great powers versus the rest (and each other). Great powers, whether they are democratic or authoritarian, will seek to influence and interfere with world affairs to their advantage. Smaller powers can hope that they're not at the end of the big stick wielded by great powers, democratic or authoritarian.

As Kassam and Lim note, one place where the jostling for influence is playing out is in international institutions. I agree that institutions are important, but for a different reason. Despite their deficiencies, they are one of the few arenas in which middle and smaller powers can resist bullying by great powers. This is why it is important for Australia, and other middle powers, to band together and support international institutions, and ensure they do not merely reflect the will of the great powers.

This is not to say we don't have to worry about China's conduct. Domestically, China's illiberal turn under Xi Jinping in recent years is increasingly threatening to peoples of the People's Republic. We are seeing ethnic minorities being oppressed and dissent being crushed.

So we should pay attention to what's going on inside China, because it affects one-fifth of the world's population. We should speak up about human rights in China, just as we should speak up about human rights everywhere, including at home.

Yet in its efforts to counter China, the Australian government has started to imitate the Chinese government in many ways. We're seeing a worrying trend towards prioritising national security over openness, transparency, civil liberties and the market economy – a trend towards illiberalism. I'm not as optimistic as the authors that Australia will remain "a liberal democracy, and a staunch defender of free markets and human rights".

We need to see all countries with clear and critical eyes, not just those with governments we don't like. Though the international order was never as liberal and open as some today like to claim, we should still promote liberal values to protect the weak against the strong at home and abroad. On this, I agree with the authors.

Yun Jiang is the producer of China Neican *and a managing editor of the* China Story *blog at the Australian Centre on China in the World, Australian National University.*

Natasha Kassam and Darren Lim respond

Hypocrisy and inconsistency are, and always will be, features of geopolitics. The powerful often claim to uphold certain values and standards, but regularly and rapidly discard these when their interests conflict.

To be effective, political orders must manage their most powerful members in productive ways. Liberal orders seek to impose limits on the most powerful. The American project is one example – through the US constitution and a network of laws, institutions and norms, the government derives its authority from the consent of the citizenry, and is constrained from wielding power arbitrarily or excessively.

That's the theory, anyway.

Donald Trump represented an existential challenge to a US political system that was already chronically sick. His policies, rhetoric and methods cut against black-letter laws and institutions, and many unwritten norms. He sought consistently to circumvent and undermine these structures.

But the system pushed back – in Congress, in the courts, in the media, and among civil society and the American public. This pushback was possible because the US system remains relatively transparent. Trump's actions were scrutinised and investigated, and many of his misdeeds brought to light.

Transparency led to accountability at the ballot box. Admittedly, it was a close call, and the Republican Party continues to trend in troubling directions. Moreover, the United States is grappling with a legacy of entrenched discrimination and inequality, and political institutions that often fail the most vulnerable. America is not out of the woods, but its struggles are on vivid display. Bearing witness to failure is an essential first step to progress.

The postwar liberal international order reflects key features of the American system. It created rules and institutions, and developed norms, with the intention of imposing constraints on the exercise of naked power.

We agree with Yun Jiang that it has often failed. Washington did not live up to its own standards, domestically and internationally, and the system was unable to serve as an effective constraint.

But high-profile failures obscure low-level, almost quotidian, successes. Today's international system is dense with structures that channel states' behaviour in productive ways. The overwhelming majority of international trade, for example, is conducted within a rules-based framework to which states have ceded a degree of their sovereignty, without controversy. This is a remarkable achievement in historical context, but one too easily taken for granted today.

Transparency is also a central pillar of the liberal international order – and this is where we disagree with Jiang when she draws an equivalence between the United States and China as great powers. While it may not constrain determined governments, transparency enables the imposition of costs – sometimes punitive, more often reputational – on those which violate the order's precepts.

China's political project takes a vastly different approach to managing the powerful. Its priority is to entrench and bolster the power and authority of the Party. There is little role for transparency. The free flow of information is a threat to the legitimacy of the Party's rule. There is accountability, but it is narrowly defined. The government draws upon a truly extraordinary apparatus of control, censorship and repression to keep it that way.

The open contest of ideas has always been challenged in Beijing, but has become more restricted in recent years. Beijing expels or detains journalists, restricts access to Xinjiang and Tibet, and imprisons those who speak out against the crushing of freedom in Hong Kong. Outside the country, those who criticise China are aggressively shouted down by Wolf Warrior officials and state media, or even sanctioned by the state.

When a truly global challenge arose in the form of COVID-19, Beijing prioritised secrecy over transparency, depriving World Health Organization investigators, and thus the world, of the full set of information needed to help fight future pandemics.

A China-led international order would not wholly overturn the current system. But it will reflect alternative principles. Some of these differences may be subtle in form, but profound in their impact. Transparency is at the top of this list.

Without transparency, there can be no scrutiny. Without scrutiny, there can be no correction, no progress.

Australia needs to promote an international order that prioritises transparency. This means playing an active role in those international institutions tasked with gathering and communicating information. It means promoting transparency and accountability within individual countries, including our own. It means supporting international civil society actors and the media as essential cogs in a liberal order. It means resisting efforts to silence, at home and abroad.

Transparency is a thorn in the side of any political actor. Successful political systems anticipate and prepare for such actors doing whatever they can to avoid or repress transparency mechanisms.

The liberal political project is the effort to design rules, institutions and other mechanisms that reflect principles other than naked realpolitik. The hard part is implementation and enforcement; to ensure that the powerful do face constraints, even when their major interests are at stake.

The project will fail again. The avowedly virtuous will cover themselves in hypocrisy. Meanwhile, repressive leaders will retain power, even win elections. Accused war criminals will avoid justice. Trump could return to the presidency. But in a system where transparency is retained, these failures can be discovered and scrutinised, debated and criticised, in the hope of seeding mechanisms of accountability.

Otherwise, in the march of autocracy, the rest is silence.

Natasha Kassam is the director of the Lowy Institute's Public Opinion and Foreign Policy Program.

Darren Lim is a senior lecturer in international relations at the Australian National University and co-host of the Australia in the World *podcast.*

Subscribe to Australian Foreign Affairs & save up to 28% on the cover price.

Enjoy free home delivery of the print edition and full digital as well as ebook access to the journal via the Australian Foreign Affairs website, iPad, iPhone and Android apps.

Forthcoming issue: India Rising? (October 2021)

Never miss an issue. Subscribe and save.

☐ **1 year auto-renewing print and digital subscription** (3 issues) $49.99 within Australia. Outside Australia $79.99*.

☐ **1 year print and digital subscription** (3 issues) $59.99 within Australia. Outside Australia $99.99.

☐ **1 year auto-renewing digital subscription** (3 issues) $29.99.*

☐ **2 year print and digital subscription** (6 issues) $114.99 within Australia.

☐ Tick here to commence subscription with the current issue.

Give an inspired gift. Subscribe a friend.

☐ **1 year print and digital gift subscription** (3 issues) $59.99 within Australia. Outside Australia $99.99.

☐ **1 year digital-only gift subscription** (3 issues) $29.99.

☐ **2 year print and digital gift subscription** (6 issues) $114.99 within Australia.

☐ Tick here to commence subscription with the current issue.

ALL PRICES INCLUDE GST, POSTAGE AND HANDLING.

*Your subscription will automatically renew until you notify us to stop. Prior to the end of your subscription period, we will send you a reminder notice.

Please turn over for subscription order form, or subscribe online at **australianforeignaffairs.com** Alternatively, call 1800 077 514 or +61 3 9486 0288 or email **subscribe@australianforeignaffairs.com**

Back Issues

ALL PRICES INCLUDE GST, POSTAGE AND HANDLING.

- [ ] **AFA1** ($15.99)
  The Big Picture
- [ ] **AFA2** ($15.99)
  Trump in Asia
- [ ] **AFA3** ($15.99)
  Australia & Indonesia
- [ ] **AFA4** ($15.99)
  Defending Australia
- [ ] **AFA5** ($15.99)
  Are We Asian Yet?
- [ ] **AFA6** ($15.99)
  Our Sphere of Influence
- [ ] **AFA7** ($15.99)
  China Dependence
- [ ] **AFA8** ($15.99)
  Can We Trust America?
- [ ] **AFA9** ($15.99)
  Spy vs Spy
- [ ] **AFA10** ($22.99)
  Friends, Allies and Enemies
- [ ] **AFA11** ($22.99)
  The March of Autocracy

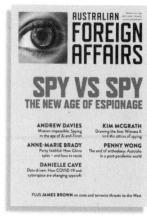

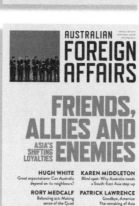

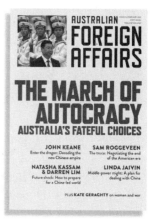

PAYMENT DETAILS I enclose a cheque/money order made out to Schwartz Books Pty Ltd. Or please debit my credit card (MasterCard, Visa or Amex accepted).

CARD NO.

EXPIRY DATE   /   CCV   AMOUNT $

CARDHOLDER'S NAME

SIGNATURE

NAME

ADDRESS

EMAIL   PHONE

Post or fax this form to: Reply Paid 90094, Carlton VIC 3053 **Freecall:** 1800 077 514 **or** +61 3 9486 0288
Fax: (03) 9011 6106 **Email:** subscribe@australianforeignaffairs.com **Website:** australianforeignaffairs.com
Subscribe online at australianforeignaffairs.com/subscribe (please do not send electronic scans of this form)

A FREE PODCAST ABOUT FOREIGN AFFAIRS IN AUSTRALIA AND THE ASIA-PACIFIC

SUBSCRIBE TODAY

AUSTRALIANFOREIGNAFFAIRS.COM/PODCAST

AFA WEEKLY

FOREIGN AFFAIRS & TRADE NEWS

A **free** weekly email from Australian Foreign Affairs journal

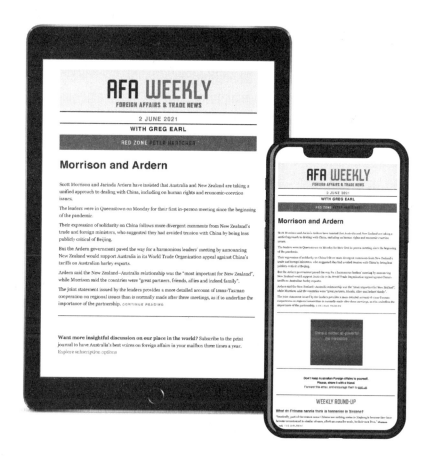

AUSTRALIANFOREIGNAFFAIRS.COM/AFA-WEEKLY

The Back Page

WOLF WARRIOR DIPLOMACY

What is it: A breed of defiant Chinese diplomats, known for their forthright or even bellicose statements. They use social media to defend China and counteract criticism with criticism of their own. *Vox* (liberal explainer website, United States) has called them "professional diplomatic trolls".

Who are they: Zhao Lijian (spokesperson, Chinese foreign ministry), known in Australia for tweeting a photoshopped image of an Australian soldier slitting an Afghan child's throat; Yang Jiechi (senior diplomat, Politburo member); and Li Yang (Chinese consul-general, Rio de Janeiro) are leading examples.

Where does it come from: Two top-grossing Chinese action films with nationalistic motifs, *Wolf Warrior* and *Wolf Warrior 2*. The original has been called "Rambo with Chinese characteristics".

Some wolf calls: Hu Xijin (editor, *Global Times*): "Australia is always there, making trouble. It is a bit like chewing gum stuck on the sole of China's shoes"; Li Yang to Justin Trudeau (prime minister, Canada): "Boy, your greatest achievement is to have ruined the friendly relations between China and Canada, and have turned Canada into a running dog of the US."

Why are they doing it: Wolf warrior diplomacy may be intended more for an audience in Beijing than beyond – it allows apparatchiks to signal their party loyalty in robust terms. Lindsay Gorman (Emerging Technologies Fellow, Alliance for Securing Democracy) says the tactic is "backfiring", at least in the West. Yuan Nansheng (vice-president, China Institute of International Studies) wrote that "the wolf warrior spirit contradicts traditional Chinese culture".